YOUNG

ENIGMA

doghornpublishing.com

Editor: Adam Lowe
Cover art by Glenn Jones
Typesetting by Adam Lowe

Published by Dog Horn Publishing, 2015

First published in the United Kingdom in 2014 by
Dog Horn Publishing
45 Monk Ings
Birstall
Batley
WF17 9HU

doghornpublishing.com

Young Enigma is grateful to Arts Council England, Commonword
and Archives+ for supporting this publication.

British Library Cataloguing-in-Publication Data
A cataloguing record for this book is available on request from the
British Library

ISBN: 978-1-907133-80-0
Printed and bound in the UK.

commonword   LOTTERY FUNDED   Supported using public funding by
ARTS COUNCIL ENGLAND

In memory of Leelah Alcorn
and all the siblings
who have left us.

Rest in power.

TABLE OF CONTENTS

INTRODUCTION

SPOKE: New Queer Voices has been in the works for a couple of years now. This book brings together some of the best young writers working today—all connected by their queer identities. *SPOKE* is the culmination of two years of Young Enigma, a writer development project designed to support new and emerging writers who identify as LGBT, and is part of our search to champion those voices. The name has a dual meaning: it references the spokes of progress, change, science and technology; but it also references the act of speaking up and speaking out. The capitalisation is intentional: we want to speak loudly. The voices here are queer—meaning more than just *gay* or *lesbian*—and the voices here, while accomplished in their own rights, are 'new' in that they're at the beginning of what we hope are spectacular careers for all involved.

Pete Kalu, Afshan Lodhi and I formed Young Enigma in October 2012. We began recruiting writers across various disciplines and sought stakeholders who might help us reach a wider audience. By January 2013, we had a group of writers that met regularly and a focus: we were the inaugural LGBT History Month Writers in Residence. Together we worked towards a series of micro commissions that would be exhibited, performed and published during LGBT History Month 2013. These included two radio plays broadcast in Manchester and nationally, a poem in *The Sunday Telegraph*'s *LGBT History Month Magazine,* live performances on Canal Street, and an interactive poetry map available in Google Maps. We also had an ebook anthology of new writing, which was the seed of this book.

Young Enigma was formed because we were aware of a gap in provision. Commonword (the writer development agency for the North West of England) wanted to create a safe space for a next generation of LGBT writers in the region. Previous LGBT groups that had met in Commonword's space, beneath the Friends Meeting House in Manchester, no longer met for various reasons. In some instances, this was because they had gone on to bigger and better things. and for others it was because the group was no longer doing what the writers needed it to. We agreed there and then that an independent group—housed by Commonword, but with its own aims and objectives, and its own constitution—would be the best way for us to forge a path of our own, while still benefiting from the support and advice Commonword could offer.

Pete, Afshan and I chatted at length about what we could do to keep such a group together, given that writing can often be a solitary task and that writers can, if left to their own devices, wander off to do their own thing. We decided, therefore, that it was best to keep the group together by offering members not only one-to-one support, but also opportunities to do things together for an audience that would hopefully grow as each of us has grown in our own writing. Nothing keeps a bunch of people together better than a call to arms—and people taking note of what you do.

We knew that there was existing provision for young writers in the North, but that this wasn't always best placed to address the often complex needs of LGBT young people. With research by LGBT Yough North West (funded by BBC Children in Need) showing that 25% of LGBT young people don't have any adults they can confide in, we knew we also wanted to create a space where young people could meet peer mentors who might inspire them and encourage them to become more involved in their communities.

Thus, we agreed to set up Young Enigma with a view to supporting young and emerging writers specifically. Our work falls into two strands. Our young writers' programme supports those aged 13-25, helping to foster creativity and generate confidence in speaking out. We work with those young writers to help them grow socially, personally and professionally, while engaging them to become more active in their communities. The net benefits include increased academic attainment, increased employability and increased socio-political agency.

Our advanced programme, meanwhile, is for dedicated emerging writers and supports those at the latter end of the young writers scale and somewhat beyond (18-35 years old), in order to create a next generation of role models and peer mentors. This latter programme allows us to support those writers who would otherwise fall through the cracks of 'new writing' provision, while addressing the issue of a lack of adult role models for young LGBT people. This latter cohort of writers (informally known as the Patterflash! collective, which means 'words', 'chatter' or 'tall tales' in Polari) can raise the profile of Young Enigma more generally, while also offering their own skills through peer mentoring schemes.

What we have ended up with is a very diverse, wide-ranging collective. We have poets, performers, MCs, singers, drag queens, journalists, copywriters, actors, academics, archivists, broadcasters, promoters, publishers, activists and those who are not quite decided yet. The only thing that links them all is their desire to write or tell stories, and a willingness to share their own progress with each other.

But Young Enigma also aims to reach beyond the boundaries of Manchester and the North of England. The Young Enigma Awards, for example, scout for new LGBT writing talent in the form of the Alan Horsfall Prize and the Barbara Burford Prize. Our LGBT History Month Writers in Residence programme raises awareness of everyday queer achievement across the school curriculum and across the breadth of human endeavour. Our sister publication, *Vada Magazine*, offers opinions, reviews and news for discerning LGBT readers across the globe. And, finally, there's this book. A sort of old-fashioned reminder that we're not just in schools and on stages, that we're not just in Manchester, and that we're not just online: our queer voices are in print between two (gorgeous) covers as well. Which means we intend to hang around a little bit longer.

SPOKE is a labour of love, but it's also absolutely necessary. We wanted to put the words and voices of a new generation of LGBT writers into a book that would stand its own on bookshelves among more 'mainstream' anthologies. With the indie press, sales are never really why we do it, but we hope this is a book that will also find some kind of audience. I wish I'd found this book when I was young. I wish I'd known there were voices writing about my experiences and speaking my language when I was a teenager. It's only now that I'm relatively 'grown up' that I've finally found a space for people like me.

This is why we bring you *SPOKE*. I hope you enjoy it.

ADAM LOWE, MANCHESTER, FEBRUARY 2015

Jamal Gerald

Biography

Jamal Gerald has been working as a writer and performance artist for seven years. He has an alter ego named 'Ms. Fabulash Jones', who draws upon the black LGBT experiences of the New York ballroom culture. He's currently in the process of completing his first one-man show titled *FADoubleGOT*, which is an autobiographical piece focussing on the discovery of pride and the banishing self-loathing.

FIERCE

I always knew I was fierce.
I knew how to walk down a street,
get eyes glued to my physique.

My fashion sense is always,
always on point.
You think Naomi Campbell is fierce?

Think again. I'm the definition.
Name plastered under the word
in bold capitals. It is I,

the shy ones envy.
Flashing on their own
when I enter the room,

cameras fall in love with me.
No need to introduce.
I just pose, and they know what to do.

Say what you want.
Be sure to back it up.
I sure as hell do.

Girl, I know I'm male.
But I can show you ladies
a thing or two.

Can't take the heat? Sasha Fierce
please, take a seat.
Or else, kiss my feet.

Try and beat the fierce one.
Where you think Madonna learnt
how to Vogue?

Watch and learn.
Always been the biggest,
the best at everything.

I got men waiting on speed dial
for me. Cause, Ms. Fabulash Jones
has taken the throne.

So, my girls always ask me:
'Do you think you're fierce?' I say:
'I don't think I'm fierce . . . I know.'

DEAR MOTHER

Dear Mother,
Remember there was never a father
figure in existence. My heart
is a bruised filter, the colour of love.
My love for you is a fire.

It hurts to see you bob your head
to those dancehall tracks
like 'Boom Bye Bye'
while Buju Banton threatens
the lives of people like your son.

It hurts to know people like you
could get pleasure when they see
a body fold into a collapsing rainbow,
brutally beaten until this thing
you call an abomination is out of him.

Leviticus says: 'If a man lies with a man
as one lies with a woman, both of them
have done what is detestable.
They must be put to death;
their blood will be on their heads.'

Because of this, I kissed
all those women, tried to convince
myself to walk forward in
a straight line. *It's just a phase!*
God still loves me.

Dear Mother,
Answer me this:
Why would I choose to be a sin?
How could I choose, when God
knitted me in your womb as I am?

Born to find a woman's curves uninviting.
Hour-glass shape just don't do it for me.
I realise that I was born to write this poem.
Yours sincerely,
Your Sin.

SCREAMER

I want your lips to taste
like gospel. Your Greek god skin
never fades.

Your eyes are forests in winter, sugar
snowflakes on emerald leaves
that shake when you blink.

I want to wrestle to your
favourite heavy metal,
and sing with the band.

I want to crack your emotions
like knuckles. With a pop. Be the wind
in motion between your thighs.

I want to grasp you. Your hair
is the black snake hunting its prey.
You are the glowing full moon.

I want the sunset. Howl so hard
we interrupt the dead's rest.
We resurrect. Scream.

BIBLE BASHERS

I used to burn Bibles as a hobby.
To help me get rid of quotes
that penned in my thoughts
with permanent ink.

I'm tired of being told
where my final destination lies.
I'm at the point where I don't care
if my soul falls or flies.

If heaven doesn't want me,
closes golden gates in my face,
then I'll happily go to Hell.
I'll descend like a proud angel.

Who are you to decide who gets a place
in Paradise? Who are you to say
this is the Word of God when you
have never heard Him speak?

I decided until I hear
these commands from His mouth
touch my so-called guilty soul,
I'm not believing a word.

CALEB EVERETT

BIOGRAPHY

Caleb Everett was born with a quill in his hand, of low income even at birth. In time this was replaced with a biro, purchased from The Works (five blue ink biros on a £1.99 offer). Since then he has written various things that no one has read and fewer have cared about. Between 2008-2010 he was the lead drinker of a London-based pop group. He is currently residing in Manchester, writing a prequel to a book that hasn't yet been published and assembling a band for the first time in three years. He has a certifiable obsession with Patti Smith, wears a size-9 court shoe and claims to have given up smoking to improve his luck on Grindr.

THE MANCHESTERFORD DIARIES

INTRODUCTION

The Manchesterford Diaries is a tale both with and without narrative. Not quite a diary—insofar as it doesn't luxuriate in personal dreariness—but it isn't glittery, imaginative fiction. It's a mischievous, organic way of telling stories. Something I've always loved doing.

The Manchesterford Diaries is my love letter to the cinematic tales of the suburbs, the bluesy all-knowing intellect of my grandparents, the vodka-sodden love of my friends, my bewildering forays into the world of small-time rock 'n' roll and . . . well, the list is as endless as a life can be on a severe budget.

The Manchesterford Diaries are taken from actual real-life-biggish-boy diaries and span from 2009-2014. It's a slim volume. The following excerpts are raffles drawn at random.

TOUR DE JUILLET

Saturday July 5th 2014, Manchester to Holmfirth:
Last of the Summer Whiners

It's 11am and I'm jolted awake by the hangover fairy. My bedroom floor is elegantly scattered with clothes, copper and an untouched portion of takeaway chips. I pick up my phone—which neglected to play my 9am alarm—and, now all a-jitter, note I have 75 minutes to tart up my pale sloth-like remains and drag my bones to Piccadilly Station.

All I crave is a day of hobbling from dimly lit room to dimly lit room; a barely-living hangover cocktail of Lady Grey, chocolate and tramadol. But I must ready myself.

I shower away the pub-stench of last night, staple my eyes back to where they once rested and studiously place Elnett upon Elnett to zhoosh up the quiff. Looking like James Dean (post-car crash) and sounding like Bonnie Tyler playing a camp Darth Vader, I resign myself to a day of teeth-clenched smiles and doing shots of Gaviscon.

On the bus. Everyone looks as glum as I do . . . which is reassuring. Someone notices I've made an effort with my hair and shouts, 'Y' alright, Elvis?' I waste my last breath on a disappointed sigh and continue scribbling out Jess' birthday card. I'm gushing compliments to excuse lack of presents this year and only stop short of claiming she's the most fabulous thing to ever exit a womb.

Someone's boarded the bus wearing pink Crocs. I need to lie down.

*

I meet Jess, and her friends Dan and Katie, at Piccadilly Station on time. Dan's wearing his hair pompadour style, wearing a fetching t-shirt of Jesus with the advice 'kill your idols' scrawled across it. Katie is all green and grins and Jess is effortlessly Jess: an admirable shift without end, she's draped in dark colours with machine-gun fire wit at the ready. She skips through the itineray for her 27th birthday do and it's now I realise I left her card on the 81. I don't mention it.

We're to be on the next train to Huddersfield, collected by her friend Charlotte and dumped at her mum's house in Holmfirth where we won't be able to move for finger food and Prosecco. Then on Sunday it's the Annual Rubber Duck Race which, this year, is somewhat overshadowed by the Tour de France passing through. I'm knee-deep in ignorance of any sporting event that doesn't heavily feature the rubber duck.

JESS: Well, how many did you offend with withering putdowns last night, Caleb?

ME: Let's see what text messages come through later and I'll answer then.

There's a group of space-hopper-shaped men on the platform squeezed into Hawaiian shirts. They're jabbering on about the Tour de France and get onto Lance Armstrong.

21

SPACE HOPPER 1: I mean, I know he were on drugs but you've still gotta admire the man.

SPACE HOPPER 2: Can't fucking stand him.

SPACE HOPPER 3: . . . and he only had one bollock.

SPACE HOPPER 1: Exactly !

We board the train. It's all exposed armpits and knockoff Lynx covering B.O. that could bring down a Boeing 747. Katie, who's lugging a booze factory about in a Co-op bag, hands us each a pear-flavoured cider and I exhale a barrel of relief.

The Yorkshire scenery comes into sight, a Salvation Army brass band wafts through the mind, and I understand the boastful nature of a Yorkshireman. These moors, slopes and sodden sheep are our own Australian Outback, where the ghosts of poets and Brontë Sisters hide from train view. We all peer through the window, at one moment or another, and are equally as taken with the landscape. The English . . . we're constantly surprised by beauty on our own welcome mat.

*

Huddersfield has the third highest number of listed buildings in the country and the fact ricochets off every brick and cobble as we leave the station. Outside the station is bustling with marquees, food stalls, picnic benches, rosy faced drunks and lycra-clad sports fans—fans of the Tour de Force rather than the Duck Race, I assume. Even the statue of Harold Wilson is grinning in the imported hot weather, so suited to us helpless smokers.

Charlotte greets us with more carrier-bag booze and ushers us all into her car. Jess takes the front seat to provide directions. As she fumbles with choice of reggae CD, Charlotte issues her travel advisory: 'You direct me, Jess . . . and please pay attention to the roads because I'm not.' At this point we pass through a red light. Dan, Katie and I double-check we're buckled up and fall into a heap of silent prayer.

We arrive in Holmfirth, known in Yorkshire as 'Little Hollywood', primarily because it's where Last of the Summer Wine was filmed for 300 years. The outside heat is wailing for our presence, Mark and Simon join and the Unholy Trinity of Queens is established for a contractual buffet of finger food, booze and nasal northern cheer. There's a quiche tin containing a few spliffs being passed around, for those interested. Jess' eyes widen like some histrionic Warner Bros. cartoon character as her mum approaches the picnic—'Shit! My mum doesn't know I smoke cigarettes. Quick! Pass me that spliff.' Nicotine laughter rocks the rafters and Jess surpasses Nora Batty in Holmfirth's comedy chart.

Sunday July 6th 2014, Holmfirth

I resurface into life at 10am and am greeted by expressions rich with hangovers. Faces teleported directly from Death Row. I feel fine but don't wish to brag with a series of cartwheels, so I scuttle into a corner and load up Grindr—the trigger-happy tool of a wounded tribe. In the most butt-clenchingly vibrant cities Grindr is, at best, like playing Supermarket Sweep around Poundland, so I'm curious what a postage-stamp-sized town will offer. The chessboard squares throw up the usual Stepford Gays, embryos in espadrilles and blurry landscape shots. There are lots of profiles with 'visitor' as headline and I even spy an ex-lover who still resembles an early-draft of a living being. I briefly chat with someone from Huddersfield who sends me a post-shower photo of himself.

HIM: What do you think, mate?

ME: Just how do you get your towels so white?

Blocked without so much as a polite 'LOL'.

*

Jess, Dan, Katie, Mark, Simon and I get ready to head to the Sands Recreation Grounds in Holmfirth. Charlotte isn't joining, as she has to be back in Leeds. Before leaving she spits out some fantastic Tour de France facts. The most memorable will remain, 'Each cyclist doing the race will sweat out the equivalent of 150, 000 toilets being flushed . . . ' Or was it 15, 000 . . . ?

Sands Recreation Grounds, and its surroundings, are unmarked by the brutal buildings that usually litter life. Even today with the children's fare, the pop-up Indian delicatessens and the cinema-sized screen the delightfulness of it remains. The most beautiful people are out today and the grass is most definitely greenest just where we are. You can't move for picnic hampers, protruding light-switch-shaped nipples and balls a-swinging under tracksuit bottoms.

*

SIMON: We'll have to go up on the hill soon to see the cyclists pass by. It's 2.30 and they're supposed to be passing through at 2.45.

Jess and I agree it's not much of a race if you know when the competitors are whizzing by but we stagger onto a viewing platform for a vada at the lycra. People are yelling out pleasantries in French and, caught up in a rare moment of enthusiasm, I join in with the first sprinkling of French that pops to mind . . . 'Je m'appelle Caleb'.

The cyclists pass. I've had vaccinations that pickpocketed more time from an afternoon and I can only hope the Duck Race makes up for the crushing disappointment of loosing our spot on the lawns.

It's now I receive a text message with a request that I get back to Manchesterford as soon as I can.

THE MOSTON DANGLER

Monday 27 January 2014

Hospital appointment for this throat infection which resolutely refuses to budge. Medical problems, no matter how trivial or severe, are as boring as sin. Though, for writers with an ear finely tuned for a Northern soundbite it can be a sterilised Aladdin's Cave.

Arrive fifteen minutes early for my appointment at 10am. Another waiting room and another bead-maze-table-toy I must resist playing with. Two elderly ladies do a crab-like shuffle to the seats facing and scan the announcement board on the faded shade-of-dull wall behind me.

One of the felt-hatted dears taps her companion on the arm. 'D' you know what I thought that said? I thought it said: "Are you tired of Domestos' abuse?" I thought, "Funny thing to have a helpline for."

Alan Bennett would kick off his court shoes, peel the cellophane from his sarnies and prepare for a long stay but I'm called in by the nurse.

*

OLDER NURSE: Hello luv. Come in and take a seat.

ME: Thank you.

OLDER NURSE: Goodness, your throat is very hoarse, isn't it?

ME: I know I sound like Deidre Barlow now but it's better than a fortnight ago . . . I sounded like an asthmatic Phyllis Pierce.

(Nurses laugh but the younger nurse is clearly baffled by the latter name.)

OLDER NURSE: She won't know who that is. How do you know who she is? That's way before your time.

ME: I was dragged up in the dressing rooms at Granada so I can natter, from arsehole to breakfast time, about *Coronation Street* from decades before I was born. Especially Pat Phoenix, who has the greatest opening line to a memoir ever—'I am a bastard.'

OLDER NURSE: *Coronation Street* would have to be my specialised subject on Mastermind. I still love it but it was much better in my day, before everyone was killing everyone over having some affair.

ME: Definitely. The women in it are so poorly written now. No high hair. No ambition beyond a deep-fat fryer. They're just constantly weeping over some man who resembles a tin of spam with a beard. I mean, who'd want to drag up as any of the women in it now?

(The older nurse and I exchange stories about favourite Corrie characters and storylines.)

YOUNGER NURSE: Ooh, I've got a claim to fame with *Coronation Street*! You remember the guy who played Jack Duckworth?

ME & OLDER NURSE: Yes.

YOUNGER NURSE: Well . . . he's buried next to my granddad.

I'm issued with a follow-up appointment for next week, when a camera will explore the throat properly. Until then I'm to speak as little as possible. I feel a popular week ahead.

*

Watching the news with Nana and Granddad. There's a segment about Bill Roache's trial. The actors who play Deirdre and Peter Barlow have been giving character references. If Blanche were still with us Preston Crown Court would have been sold out for months.

GRANDDAD: Fat lot of good they are for a character reference. He's an alcoholic and she's cheated on him god knows how many times.

Nan rolls her eyes.

Tuesday 28 January 2014

Feeling mortified, just like a good lapsed Catholic should.

Earlier today Nan let the golden skinned window cleaner, Daz, in to use the loo. He's a tracksuited Triga Porn dream. Gold chains, bad tattoos, Lynx knockoff and Adidas sportswear, which make him look like a sexy living barcode. He's all anyone could ever want to fill the lonely hours between Jeremy Kyle and *Loose Women*. Moston's own George Formby with an ASBO, who treats his love to 3-for-£5 Blue WKDs after his window cleaning round.

I'm unaware Daz is in the house, as I'm bundled in the shower. The windows were cleaned hours ago so I've no reason to lock myself in a coffin to avoid drooling over a scally with a shammy. Daz uses the toilet and strides over to the bathroom. I've just wrapped a towel around my waist. The door opens (dodgy council-fitted lock) and in pops the Adonis in Adidas, not in the least bit embarrassed.

'Ah sorry mate. Just need to wash me hands. Good job ya got a towel on, eh?' He laughed, which thankfully muffled the sound of my ovaries sighing. Then, in a somewhat dazed state I said, 'I would've trimmed if I knew I was going to have company.'

So. Embarrassed.

Michael Brown,
aka Poet Brownie

Biography

One of the original members of Young Enigma and a 2013 LGBT History Month Writer-in-Residence, Poet Brownie is something of a prodigal son of Manchester's. He was known for years as a key face on the poetry and performance scenes with his particular brand of poetry, song and comedy.

One of my favourite memories of Brownie is when he performed a live rendition of 'Gay Pregnant Man' on Canal Street during Young Enigma's *Pride & Prejudice: A Poetry Parade*—a kind of literary pride parade through Manchester's Gay Village. It's not often that the customers of Canal Street get to see a queer poet giving birth to his own T-shirt outside what was then Queer (and is now Kiki). It was certainly lots of fun!

His new collection, *The Exhibit,* was recently published by Silverwood Books. You can find out more about Poet Brownie and his work at poetbrownie.com.

GAY PREGNANT MAN

It's not great
I'm putting on weight
Got a craving for cake

Can gay guys get pregnant these days?
Went to Boots Pharmacy, got a test
Went to Arndale bogs, took a piss

Sign of the cross

I'm pregnant
Up the duff
Bun in oven
With child

Don't know who the Father is
Probably some guy I met off Grindr
Serves me right

I like it bareback
So he probably left the condom off
Anyway it is Saturday night—I'm still going out
Tenner in my pocket, I'm going to town
With me friends Dan and Matty
We're going Essentials

I'm on the dance floor and . . .
My waters have broke
Is there a doctor in the house?
Preferably one who is gay and attractive
Like him off *Embarrassing Bodies* on the telly
Call an ambulance

No I ain't OD'd

I'm pregnant
Up the duff
Bun in oven
With child

I'm rushed to Hospital
But there's a nun there
'Cause there's always nuns in hospitals

She says:
'Gays shouldn't have children,
It's unnatural. It will turn out to be
The Devil's child!'
Oh . . . probably be a little Goth boy
We'll call him Damien.

James Hodgson

Biography

James Hodgson is okay. He has a PhD in Brazilian films from the 1970s and works in an office. He writes short stories and the odd poem; he has been published in a few places for the latter. He likes Adam Marek, Andrew Holleran and bits of Dennis Cooper. He is okay, okay.

SCORPION

Shimmering beneath a desk, square between Michael Amstridge's shoes, Frank first thought the scorpion was a figurine cut from rock crystal similar to those collected by middle-aged women, and that Michael must have dropped it by accident. Frank looked up at the fine hairs on the back of Michael's neck. He wanted to say something but knew the consequences were he to speak prematurely—Michael might laugh at his kindness, or jump back in surprise and crush the scorpion beneath his feet—and anyhow, the scorpion had started to move curiously from left to right, clicking on the laminate, so Frank quickly decided it was a hallucination and that he would say nothing. When the room emptied and the multitude of smells and hormones departed, Frank crouched beneath the desk to look for it, but the insect had already scurried away.

Frank told himself that most people probably see stuff they don't understand once or twice in their life, and that it was nothing to worry about. It would be best to put it behind him.

*

Frank saw the scorpion again a few weeks later. The class was getting ready for football practice—fifteen or so year 10s shivering in grim changing rooms, mentally preparing for competition. The scorpion shone out from beneath a shin-pad. It looked right at him.

Frank bit his thumbnail. Watching Pete Smalls unbutton his shirt, he knew he should point it out and confirm, once and for all, whether the arachnid existed purely in his mind or if it was a real thing in itself. He knew the words existed; he could feel them on his tongue.

Frank and Pete shared a row of hooks at the back of the room, which meant Frank could whisper and no one would cotton on if Peter reacted in a bad way. He readied himself.

'Pete—'

Pete looked up. His shirt was nearly unbuttoned all the way. Just as Frank was about to say something, the transparent creature waved its sting like a jewelled earring. A warning. He held back.

'Are you alright?' Pete asked. Frank nodded and let the scorpion slip away into the recesses of his sport bag. He was filled with the urge to crush it.

The PE teacher called them out to the field. Watching the stragglers jog out onto the pitch, Frank knew for certain he had lost before the game even began.

*

Nothing really happened for a long time after that. Frank got on with life, kept to himself and did his homework. He dreamed about things that left him confused and sweating. One dream featured a grand and beautiful theatre continually flooded by a tropical ocean—from which Frank woke with an inexplicable sadness. His first thoughts tied any explanation of strangeness back to the scorpion. He waited for it under the sheets and grew nervous.

A few routes of action might have changed his situation, of course: he could tell his parents, for one, although he was sure that they would see the scorpion as a sign of incipient schizophrenia. Visual hallucinations always meant madness to those who didn't have to see them.

Occasionally Frank imagined his life as a mad person. He'd only ever known mad people through movies and books, so his fantasy was one of slow decline, supported by medication and sympathetic but controlling psychiatrists.

Sometimes Frank thought he could run away from home and join an artist's commune, where he was certain other schizophrenics might be found, but he was afraid they might think him pretentious. Instead, he said nothing. He found himself sketching the insect inside the cover of his homework planner. He looked up different breeds online, but nothing quite matched it. It remained a mystery.

*

Frank didn't know how long he'd been waiting. My god, he'd been waiting forever. Just as they got into the third act the studio lights had suddenly gone off and the production crew and stage-hands started running around trying to fix things. The actors stood still, trying their best to keep their cool and not think about the delay or what the reviews might look like. The orchestra conductor told the first and second clarinets to start from the first scherzo. They, too, had been waiting for a long time.

When the clarinets began, the ceiling opened up to a dark sky filled with stars. Clouds drifted slowly above. Frank thought it was an obvious way to distract the audience, but they fell for it and cooed with delight.

The lights came on and the audience applauded, but the celebrations were cut short when the lights started to flash erratically. It was as if the system had been hooked up for a different show and the theatre received their signals by mistake.

Then, as a few stray members of the audience began to stand to leave, the rear theatre wall fell back to reveal a tropical ocean. Small coral atolls peppered the horizon. A sandbar swept up to the theatre, providing an easy route into paradise for those prepared to wade. The moon hung close to the horizon. The orchestra played on.

A tall tree broke through the wall with the sound of snares tumbling over. A monkey came down and began throwing pieces of bark at the audience. The audience was still mostly unmoved, preferring to focus on the music rather than the strange events around them. Frank started laughing. The play was completely ruined—why were these people still watching?

Several parties, it seemed, had finally reached the same conclusion, and they stormed out just as a river of seawater began to flow over the stage. The first two rows of people began screaming like their lives were in real danger, only to be shushed by the remaining audience as they strained to listen to the orchestra—an orchestra that continued despite the chaos.

The orchestra completed the first scherzo to the conductor's satisfaction. He raised his hands to move onto the next section. Mist poured in from the left wing of the stage but neither he nor the musicians noticed.

Lobelias and ivy spread up into the boxes. An extra rolled his trousers around his thighs and sparked up a cigarette. Another monkey jumped onto the stage and started to unpick the floorboards, only to *discover wet sand beneath.*

A series of powerful waves washed most of the proscenium arch off into the ocean, each assault curling over and collapsing on the stage, washing the stalls with white froth and soaking the orchestra's music. One by one the players gave up until the last clarinet threw her instrument into the sea and ran off, sobbing. With no music and a rapidly dwindling band of actors, the complaints grew louder, but most of the audience seemed unwilling to leave the theatre.

Eventually, the producer appeared and began to apologise.

'The stage-manager ran off with someone from ticket sales, apparently.' So that was the root cause of the problem—an errant stage-manager. Most of the audience bought this.

'If you proceed down to the sea front, we'll carry out the final act of the play on the beach.' He pointed at a stretch of golden-white sand that shone despite the night. 'And we'll refund the tickets of any patrons who haven't found the play to their satisfaction.'

A sea-turtle laid a cluster of eggs in the sand right next to Frank, covering them up with a flipper before disappearing into the spray.

Frank was glad—he wanted very much to see the final act, although he couldn't be sure why. So it will all be worth it in the end, won't it? It'll always comes right in the end, *he thought. He had been waiting for this for so long.*

Most of the audience headed into the stalls, which were waterlogged and festooned in shreds of seaweed, at which point the producer organized everyone into a long line and told them to wait their turn.

Frank watched everyone else run into the water. A colony of tropical ferns pushed out through the first floor boxes. The crowd started shuffling in line.

'Finally!' Frank said. 'Do you know how long I've been waiting?'

He tapped the shoulder of the woman in front, who wore a velvet dress.

'Do you know how long I've been waiting?'

She looked at him, then she repeated his words back to him, laughing. He laughed too.

The crowd moved steadily up to the edge where the sea met the stage. The paradise shone beyond and cast a blue-green light on the remnants of the stalls.

'Do you know how long I've been waiting?' Frank said again, to a man behind him. The man looked at him and laughed. They shuffled up closer to the edge, in one long line.

As the queue shuffled forward, Frank could finally see what all the fuss was about. Two men—production assistants, probably—took the lady's hand. At first, he thought they were conducting baptisms.

The two men brought her slowly under the water and held her there. She struggled near the end. After about five minutes they let go and pushed her body into the sea.

The two men were naked and beautiful.

The two men held on to Frank on either side.

Water covered his body. The two men held him down. They were powerful and gentle. After twenty seconds or so he started to panic. Frank hadn't expected this. No one told him it would be like this. He thought it would be different. The water was very cool. This wasn't how it was supposed to be at all.

*

The scorpion appeared a third time when Frank was at a party. The parents of the hostess, a girl who liked him because he was quiet, owned an enormous house with a wood at the bottom of the garden. She had lit tealights around the porch and hung streamers from the eaves, which made the place feel like a scene from a catalogue. The party was populated by sixth formers and most of them were already drunk when he arrived.

Frank felt his initial awkwardness melt as he worked his way through a mug of neat Martini Extra Dry. He talked to a few friends and tried to blend in. At about 10 o'clock, he watched the hostess run down the grass with Tom Simpson and head into the woods. Dangling unseen, the scorpion clung tightly to Tom's polo shirt with a magnificent opal claw. By then, Frank was starting to get really messed up. He went after them, stumbling on the grass and tripping over his own feet.

As he reached the edge of the wood, the scorpion dropped from Tom's shirt and scurried off. Frank set out after it. Screwing his eyes together, he tried to focus on the forest around him but the alcohol blurred tree into shrub, leaf litter into bramble, soil into root. Not so for the scorpion, which shone like a pearl as it darted this way and that, burrowing beneath mounds of deciduous leaves before reappearing again a few metres away. Frank could see it perfectly. He longed for a jar or a bag—something to hold it and preserve it as evidence.

Frank could hear Tom Simpson grunt up ahead. He ducked. The couple fell into the undergrowth. Frank tried to quieten his footsteps.

For a second he thought he lost it. The scorpion flaunted its own capacity for a smooth evasion. Flickering here, then gone, then ten metres away. Stumbling forward, Frank groped at the leaf litter in the hope he might snare the creature through sheer luck. It vanished again and left him in the dark, in silence. Frank could see Tom and the girl up ahead, cosseted within the bushes. They began to fuck.

Returning to the hunt, he realised he was lost without the light of the scorpion and almost gave up until he saw it scamper down into a ditch. He followed it. The ditch actually served as the outlet for a storm pipe, and Tom was fucking the hostess in the vegetation right above the entrance. Frank crept towards them, certain they wouldn't hear so long as he took his time to place his feet tenderly on the wet leaves.

The girl squealed. Frank froze, convinced he was discovered, but Tom kept going. He wondered if she knew what she sounded like. Frank was sure Tom was hurting her. The air got colder in the tunnel and Frank could see his own breath. The alcohol was getting to him; he felt submerged.

The scorpion glimmered in front of him before disappearing. Frank felt it wanted him to do something, make some kind of move, but he didn't understand what. He thought of the muscles in Tom's thighs bunching together and then unbunching, over and over, and how so much of her experience would depend on their capacity to sustain a rhythm. He wondered what Tom looked like, how he compared, what he would do if he were in her position.

He knelt down in front of the pile of leaves. He kept thinking of drowning, although this time he was drowning in the booze, which rose up from his throat to choke him. Coming to his senses, Frank waited for the scorpion to taunt him again. The creature flashed in and out, here and there, as if it were made of liquid metal. Finally it was still. It looked at him with twenty tiny eyes.

He held his breath, and then lunged, bringing his right hand around before using his left to snatch it up. He caught the scorpion in one sweep. He could feel it between his palms.

Frank thought he saw movement near the entrance to the tunnel. *Shit.* Had Tom finished with the girl? What would he say if he was discovered—would Tom get angry, call him a pervert, maybe even fight him? Frank held himself totally still for a few seconds.

What would Tom say if he told him about the creature?

He heard another moan. They were still fucking.

Frank sat down in the leaf litter and opened his hands.

There—he saw it in all its weird magnificence. It was motionless: its body like a pearlescent finger, with armour cut into plates that ended in elegant, useless thorns. Who knew how beautiful such a small thing could be? Its claws were inlaid with a maze of fleur-de-lys. A part of Frank wanted to protect it—to take it into his arms as you might rescue a weak animal from a predator. But the sting hung just as still as the rest of it. If he didn't act now, and act forcefully, Frank was sure he would fall to its venom. He had to destroy it.

Frank stumbled briefly but caught himself. What did the scorpion mean? He didn't know. *Visual hallucinations* are *a sign of incipient schizophrenia,* he thought. At the very least the creature was something rare and magical that had appeared, like an imaginary friend, out of nowhere. Perhaps it was a spirit animal. And even if it didn't mean anything, what should he do? If he wanted, he could kill it right there by holding the sting and breaking the body up with his fingers.

Tom and the girl were reaching their climax. Frank wanted to see Tom's face, to know what he would look like, to watch him feel what he was feeling. He placed the scorpion on his stomach and lay back, slowly. They were close now, right at the edge of orgasm. The scorpion did nothing, for a moment, then began to walk up his chest and onto his chin. Frank was shaking.

Nearby, Tom came with a series of gruff shouts. Frank could feel the scorpion's forelegs press into his lip. He closed his eyes.

Ushiku Crisafulli

Biography

Ushiku Crisafulli is a poet, playwright, actor, artist, musician, and founder of the OpenMind Collective. He co-wrote and starred in the January 2008 Manchester Playwrights Forum production of *A Last Cry* at Contact Theatre. He is part of the Contact Young Actors' Company Alumni and was Manchester's representative in Contact Theatre's Contacting the World Festival Youth Leadership summit in 2010. He was winner of the penultimate Poetry Pillow as his 'Bidaman' persona, O2 Think Big funding and the Prince's Trust Community Cash Award. He is currently working on a sci-fi theatre show called *Avant Goa'uld*, and a comedy album called *Silly Semantics*.

Return from Apathy

I.

I been on a sabbatical
you been cutting fanatical.
Chose to remain in the shadows
my silence was tactical.

II.

I'm a lone wolf living in a nation of sheep
tired of being awake while so many sleep.
My future was bleak, enclosed without hope
Now my CPR flows both articulate and dope.

III.

It wasn't the unemployed that sold us a lie,
it wasn't the disabled that left the cold to die.
It wasn't the elderly that led us to recession,
or the immigrants that gave workfare their blessing.

Rebecca Swarray

Biography

Rebecca Swarray had a previous life teaching 'A' Level Drama and Performing Arts, but took a sabbatical for eight years in favour of an alternative career in accounting. Having recently reignited her creative side, she has decided to explore writing for performance and musicality. A humorous, expressive and enthusiastic individual, Rebecca is ready and charged for the new and exciting challenges that await her.

Note

Rebecca presents a map here, written with Barnaby Callaby (see p.287). This is a poetic journey through Manchester city centre which maps onto a more consumerist vision of the city.

Do you want a cookie with that love?
Supersize or savour every crumb?
I can't eat!
I'm watching one's figure.
I've eaten!

Do you want a cookie with that love?

Yes.
Probably could manage a bit more.
Ok, could work out tomorrow.

Devouring every crumb.

It was one minute to   at

You Are Here.
Said somewhere on the

Festival ego,
4 million pound acoustics.

Edges made for   wall bound theatre.
Corners to thrust into   and fill like the blues.

Strauss's voice,
The agenda of the Danube.
Waltz me taut - version of myself.

Map by Barnaby Callaby

Fit / :twice a day
Extremely well presented / glances
Please take a seat / constantly on the move
Professional driven/ rigid in every sense
Treats / Self-treats / gobbles every mouthful.

Relaxation comes hard - always tense
Take a breath/ break - it's ok to exhale:
The gym will be there tomorrow.

Central.

inst the day, stubborn flagpoles declaring a wind.

g me the language I don't understand

g in the voice unfamiliar

your melodies lack feeling.

I will interpret you.

ging a hundred ways
Harmony to me
it's losing our rhythm.

I cannot find my place.

and Rebecca Swarray

JANE BRADLEY

BIOGRAPHY

Jane Bradley is the founder and director of For Books' Sake, a charity championing writing by women; and a writer whose fiction has been published in the UK and USA. She has performed solo at live lit events in London and Manchester, and as part of a group with Young Enigma in Manchester and at Edinburgh Fringe.

MAZDA

Things turning ugly. Happens all the time. Ever since Char hit sixteen. She's so gorgeous it makes everything else ugly. Especially the men. Always wanting what they can't have. Before long, it turns them into monsters. And that always ends in trouble.

And now Chardonnay's slumped in the backseat of their stolen silver Mazda, bundled up in her white bikini and fake-fur leopard-print coat. Caramel skin, sun-bleached blonde hair. Every inch the retro bombshell, except she's unconscious and caked with mud and blood.

Twin headlamps tunnel into the night. We're miles away from the beach by now. Miles from anywhere. But it's still not safe to stop.

'Oi. Char.' She groans from the backseat. Still beautiful, despite the matted hair and smudged make-up.

'Don't go to sleep, Char.' In the rear view mirror I see her lift her head and open one eye. She mumbles something. The words dribble into each other.

'What?'

'I said wake up.'

'Too late. I'm dead.' She's blurred around the edges, but she seems unhurt. She peels herself up off the seat.

'Brit?'

'Yeah?'

'Where are we?'

'No idea.'

'Where are we going?'

'Don't know.' A beat. Her eyes are baby-blue marbles, strobed by the streetlamps and rolling in their sockets. I watch her in the mirror, worry itching in every cell. My knuckles tighten white on the wheel. She peers at me now, fighting to focus her gaze.

'Brit?'

'Yeah?'

'I didn't know you could drive.'

'I can't.'

She sighs and leans her head against the window. We're low on petrol and I start to slow down. We're past Perpignan now. Not far from Spain, say the signs.

*

Wait. Hold up. Rewind. Let's start over. A little scene-setting first, you know?

Picture this: Char on a sun-lounger, in her white bikini with the straps undone. They make me think of licking her tan-lines. Taste the salt on her skin when we've been swimming down the beach. She's got a plastic cup of cherries and ice cubes propped on her stomach, balanced between hipbones that jut up like fins. She's fishing them out with juice-stained fingers; popping them between her lips. I'm on my front on the next sun-lounger along, in black bikini bottoms and creamy coconut-scented factor fifteen.

At home, Char's freckles are all but invisible. Here they splatter her skin like spilt paint. It's been about an hour we've been sunbathing by the pool, and we've already sunk six strawberry daiquiris each. We're not staying in this hotel though, or anywhere at this resort. We're at the hostel in the old quarter of town, sharing a bunkbed in the dorm. Or we would've been, except we're never there at night. That's the thing about Char. She never sleeps at night. Says it's a waste of time. Time we could be using to get trashed, get fucked, have fun. Sleeping's only for after sex, or when the sun is up.

So we sleep during the day, but it's better that way. We've been all over in the last few weeks. Paris, Prague, Barcelona, Amsterdam and Ibiza. City to city with sunburnt shoulders and blisters from our rucksack straps. Cheap booze, cheap drugs, good clubs. Started out sophisticated, with croissants and hot chocolate in a cafe by the river. Char memorising the lyrics to 'Lady Marmalade' on the Eurostar. I can speak some French, but not enough, and once we'd been to the top of the Eiffel Tower there was nowhere to go but on.

*

We don't pay for ourselves unless there's no other option, but even so the money we've got won't last forever. We'll have to head home

49

soon. I keep trying to convince Char we could carry on; con our way into enough cash to pay for a few more weeks, and beyond that, another adventure. She's always saying she wants to go across America in a pink Corvette, sunglasses and headscarf like Thelma or Louise, Imelda May on the stereo as loud as it'll go. Getting our kicks on Route 66. I'm picturing it already as I sink into sleep.

But Chardonnay's making eyes at the pool boys. They're sweating chorizo and Corona, and they've had her in their sights since our first day. When I wake up, they're circling like mosquitoes. She knows what she's doing when it comes to seduction. She's jailbait chic but blasé about it: cocky, classy and self-assured. Bad news for anyone she sets her sights on. Once she's got you suckered, there's no escape. Not even for me. But I've got the knowledge the others don't have. I know her mind and body better than anyone. My best friend, my cherry bomb, my evil twin.

*

'Babe.'

The engine's grumbling now, a whine coming through the steering wheel, humming through my hands. I look up to see what she wants. Char's sitting upright, coffee-coloured gazelle legs stretched out sideways on the seat. Sandy bare feet and toes painted with purple glitter polish. Bruises blooming on her thighs. Mud and blood flaking from her skin. Her eyes meet mine in the mirror.

'Yeah?'

'You know this car is shit, right?'

I try to keep my face straight, but the laugh comes bubbling up before I can swallow it down.

'You're lucky you're not bound and gagged in the boot, on your way to some psycho's sex dungeon.'

'Please,' she says, and though her words are still slurred, she seems to be past the worst. 'No self-respecting psychopath would be seen dead in this.'

I roll my eyes, and the engine's grizzling again, getting louder with every mile like the clunking coming from the boot. We're pushing a hundred on the speedometer, but on the fuel gauge the

50

needle's shivering over the E. I want to tell her she's the fucking psycho, she could've been dead in the back of their shit silver Mazda if I hadn't intervened, but I don't. Now's not the time.

So I bite back the words and give her another encouraging grin, tell her I'm sorry I couldn't do better, that next time I'll make sure our means of transportation meets her high standards. But for now we'd better settle for getting some petrol.

'Next time?' she repeats, suppressing a snort, and her voice has that edge of exhaustion, of spent emotion and being too tired to care. 'Next time I get to drive. And choose the wheels.' She curls like a cat on the seat, leans forward and puts her paws on my shoulders, frilling her fingers over my collarbone, then the knot at the back of my neck. Ten kilomètres to the next service station. On the control panel, lights tick off and on in the dark, and I've no idea what they mean. Char goes quiet again and I look up to see if she's still awake, but her eyes are wide open, cool blue and blank.

At the service station, we ransack the glove compartment and come away with a battered atlas, a fistful of coins, a black baseball cap and a pair of mirrored aviator shades she says make me look like I'm in a bad action film.

'Charming,' I tell her through gritted teeth, and bundle her blonde hair up under the cap. She stays in the car while I go inside, the sky fading like a bruise from black back to purple and blue. Neither of us wears a watch, and I turned our phones off hours ago, but you can tell morning's coming despite the dark. The stars are scrubbed and quiet and the service station is alive with light, glowing like a spaceship in a spaghetti maze of slip roads that don't lead anywhere.

I use the bathroom and come back with a wad of wet toilet paper so she can scrub off the worst of the mess. We've lost anyone who might've been following us—I hope—but even so. No need to invite awkward questions. Then we go back in together. Pay four euros for a shower so hot it scalds, in a cubicle definitely too tiny for two. Banged elbows, wet hair, soap suds blobbing onto the tiles and sand crusting around the drain. White triangles over her tits and the tanned skin in-between; her bruises blue, green and yellow, flaring from sickly to tropical when the fluorescents flicker. The water shuts off automatically when our time is up, but not before she kisses me again; my tongue in her mouth and my hands on her hips and her back pressed hard against the taps.

Back in the car, we dig through our backpacks for cleanish clothes, wriggle into shorts and t-shirts with still-wet skin, then feed change into the coffee machine and drink with the doors open while the sun comes up, maps spread out over our knees.

*

Back by the pool, there's two of them talking to her when I wake up: one on each side like she's the queen and I'm not surprised at all. There's something about them that makes me uneasy, even though one's got the glint in his eye I usually like. Their smiles are wide, full of small sharp teeth.

I'm still craving Nico, who we spent a week with in Barcelona; the only one on our entire trip who'd been able to keep up with Char and me. He had hair like an oil slick and two gold teeth, muscled arms snaked in nineties tribal tattoos and a dick that seemed to stay hard for days. 'Like George Clooney in *From Dusk 'til Dawn*,' Chardonnay had sighed, naked in his bed while he was downstairs making breakfast, 'but probably more of a bastard.' I'd swatted her with a pillow then, and pulled her close, luxuriating in having her all to myself.

No one had ever made me come like that before. Not even Char.

But the jealousy always starts creeping in eventually, so we decided to move on. Filmed all three of us fucking and left him a copy to remember us by.

So I'm cold shouldering these two to start with, even when they sneak us a bottle of tequila and two wraps of speed, bundled up in clean towels that they leave on our sunloungers when we go for a swim. We're in the turquoise water, ropes of pearl bubbles tangled between our limbs, and I'm spacing out from the cocktails and the lack of sleep, slapping Char's hands away when she inches them up my thighs, fingers snagging on elastic.

She sulks when I push her away, but not for long. Not when she's so spoilt for other options. Not with the drink and the drugs and the poolside area slowly emptying, the sun starting to sink lazy and red behind palm trees and candy-striped parasols stained with sand and salt. Not when she's got them wrapped round her finger and they're promising they know of a wild party they could take us to. *Une fête sauvage*, they say, grinning when Char laughs and makes them say it again, repeating it back and forth in daft approximations of each other's accents until they're cackling too, and it takes me a minute to realise they're even more wired than we are.

'Hear that, Britney? These two have got our night all planned out. A savage party, right?' she says, looking back at them, and they nod. They're getting cockier by the minute. The speed's making her manic, her bikini straps are slipping lower with every laugh and lopsided shrug of her shoulders, and you'd have to know her the way I do to know it's not accidental. Savage is about right for Chardonnay, and even though I'm not entirely convinced about these two jokers, the tequila's made me reckless, curling through my cells, synapses sparking from the amphetamines. When he's not talking to Char, the one with dimples is shooting me the occasional crooked smile that goes straight to my cunt. I give Chardonnay a nod, then down the rest of my drink.

*

It might be the bump on the head, but once we're back on the road, Char gets edgy again, convinced we're being followed by the police, our parents, the others that we've fucked or fucked over since we've been away. Altercations and assignations ending with cash and credit cards stuffed into underwear, melting away before they wake up, before they find out. I've always got an exit strategy. But when it comes to Char, always isn't always good enough.

She's argued me into stroppy silence, told me it's her turn to drive. But she's all over the road and I'm starting to panic. Her paranoia is contagious and I've got a fever each time she lurches between lanes.

'Watch it, Char, you're gonna get us killed.'

'Stop being a pussy, we're fine.' She spits the words, hysteria in her words as she checks the mirror again. No one for miles—it's still too early—but she keeps looking back, muttering to herself that we can't let them catch up.

I have to wrestle her off the road in the end: crocodile tears and a tussle for the wheel, then her gnawing her nails and scowling from the passenger seat in a lay-by somewhere near Pollestres. Demanding to know what we're going to do.

When I can't give her any answers, she puts the stereo on. Joan Jett, full blast. I love rock 'n' roll. I hate myself for loving you. And I don't give a damn about my bad reputation. I turn my phone back on and make a call, tell him we're in trouble. Before long, we've got a plan. With me back behind the wheel, we burn rubber towards the border. The engine's growling again, but the banging from the boot has stopped.

*

It's a party on the beach that they take us to, Dimples driving and me up front beside him. Chardonnay and Christophe rattle around in the back, snuffling their way through another packet of white powder, screeching with laughter at every bump in the road, their hands all over each other.

There's a bonfire burning by the time we arrive, magic green flames from the copper nails in the wood. Rock ballads warp through battered speaker stacks, and further down the shore the waves shush and fizz against the rocks. The tide's on its way in, they tell us, but never comes up this far. The dark's pressing down, gulping us up. Before long, I've lost sight of Chardonnay, and Dimples has me by the hand, tugging towards the dunes.

There are other conjoined couples half-hidden at intervals in the sandy hollows, but by the flickering light this far from the bonfire they're no more than silhouettes, black shadows against silver sand. The sand crunches and hisses underneath us, and I love the bite of salt against my skin. Until Dimples is licking his way down my neck and across my collarbone, and then I'm too distracted to care.

Before I wrap my legs around his head, he gives me his jacket to lie on. *Vous êtes un vrai gentleman*, I tell him, in a tone that's supposed to be flirtatious and playful, but also sort-of-sarcastic. But his mouth is already on me by then and I feel his chuckle shudder through me from the inside out.

The first time he slams his cock inside me is the first time I hear Char scream.

But my brain is fogged by Dimples, his body bucking against me and his breathing hard and fast. It takes a few moments for the sound to register—the booze and drugs have bent time into slow-mo, but only inside my head. Outside, everything's hurtling on like it was before; Dimples' back and shoulders are clawed to smithereens, his hips like pistons, so hard that for a dazed split-second I wonder whether I'll get swallowed by the sand.

Rewind. Fast-forward. Freeze-frame. Dimples juddering against me with a muffled groan and a string of French swearwords, biting my shoulder and pulling my hair. Every nerve ending alight and adrenaline surging. But somewhere in-between, the sound comes again. And this time there's no mistaking it.

I disentangle myself and climb to my feet, snatching up the jacket and zipping it over my unbuttoned shirt. Dimples is somewhere behind me, orgasm-dazed and slow. But Chardonnay's shout came from close by, so I'm stumbling down the dune to find her.

Christophe is well on the way to bleeding out by the time I get there, and I go into slow motion again. He's bare-chested, in only his jeans with the fly buttons gaping and a gash in his side, using Char's dress to try to stem the flow. Red on red, except that with only the stars to see by his blood looks more like oil.

It's on her hands and knees as well, but her white bikini looks weirdly pristine, glowing in the gloom. She's kneeling over him, and he's a mess: mannequin-eyed with a plastic sheen to his face, swearing in French and lashing out as much as he can while keeping his makeshift compress in place.

I don't see the switchblade for the first few minutes. Too busy fussing over Chardonnay, calming her mania with soothing words I definitely don't believe and examining the bloodied clot on the back of her head from a bang against a rock during their scuffle. But when I do, the slow-mo sharpens back into real-time.

I manage to get them to the car park.

Fumble through the jacket pockets.

Keys.

Ignition.

Start the car.

Get on the gas and don't look back.

She says it was self-defence. An accident. But she wouldn't let me call an ambulance.

*

We follow Nico's directions to a garage on the outskirts of Le Perthus. They're buddies of his, he says, and used to dealing with situations like this. They can take care of the car; strip it down and sell it for parts, or scrap it entirely if it's worth more that way. When we pull up at Auto Ciel & Enfer, I'm anxious, but he's promised it's all sorted, so I start rummaging through the mess we've made of the car, cramming everything back into our rucksacks. Chardonnay's been causing chaos on the backseat; it looks like a jumble sale. Clothes. Cash. Passports. Bikinis, sunglasses and perfume bottles. We've already ditched the drugs and anything that could be construed as a weapon. Shouldn't have any trouble if we get searched.

Slurping juice from a carton, Char gets out and stretches her legs. There's music blaring from somewhere inside, but no one in sight. Rolled-up silver shutters, shells of cars on cinder blocks, and a sun-puddled bench surrounded by fag-ends. We loiter for a moment, uncertain. The rear bumper is mottled dark red with rust. I trail a hand over it and it comes off in flakes. There's no sad goodbyes for Char and the shit silver Mazda. She doesn't look back as she slinks towards the bench. I shoulder my rucksack and follow.

Turns out the garage is run by Maria, a lush Latina woman with gun-metal gray eyes, grimy overalls that don't do a thing to disguise her curves, and hands covered in engine grease. Her smile makes me imagine her finger-painting her way round my body, but there's no time for that now.

When she whistles, her brother comes loping from a back office and collects the keys. He grins, but in a way that makes me feel like a badass babe and not a piece of meat. I'm wondering whether we give off a vibe now, like we're not to be messed with. Or maybe Nico just mixes with a better class of criminal than the scum that we've been used to.

They confer in whispered Spanish about the best course of

action. Chardonnay and I wait; shy, awkward, shading our eyes. Dizzied by the situation and the sun. Then Maria directs us inside, to the battered settee wheezing stuffing from a gash on one of its arms,. Espresso machine and fridge. Logbooks, auto manuals, paperwork. A lurid spraypaint mural of cartoon devils and angels doing battle on the whitewashed walls. Char's quiet but affable, links her arm through mine and ushers me into the shade.

As we disappear from sight, I hear the wince of lock and metal, and I know without looking that they're opening the boot.

Inside, Char slips off her shoes and rucksack, wastes no time in raiding the fridge. She throws me a peach and takes another for herself, then hurls herself onto the sofa with an arm over her eyes and juice dribbling down her chin. I dig through the bags for make-up, then wash my face in the tiny sink. The bathroom light flickers and buzzes firefly-bright. Breathe in. Mascara, lipstick, powder. My hands and face don't feel my own. Breathe out.

Before long, there's the sickly crunch and howl of machinery. Char's been dozing, but when the noise starts up she scrambles upright too, bunny-frantic and afraid.

'What the hell is that?'

I know the answer. I'd seen it on the way in. Realised then that it might be where our shit silver Mazda met its end. I swallow, cross to the counter and pour another cup of coffee. Keep my voice neutral and tell her.

'It's the car. Going into the compactor.'

She flumps back onto the settee and keeps her eyes closed until it goes quiet.

Soon, they shout us back into the sun and Char bums a smoke from Maria's brother while she shucks herself out of her overalls, then gives us a lift into town.

At El Petit Elefant Rosa, we order creamy piña coladas, sip them through curly plastic straws. Try not to look conspicuous.

Nico comes to collect us a in cherry-red jag with the windows rolled down; polished walnut interior thrumming warm to the touch, almost as if it's alive.

'Now this is what I call a car,' Char says, bounding into his arms and then the backseat. Borrowed from a friend, he explains, as his tattooed arms wrap round me and lift me off the ground. Just in case there's trouble. But he says this nice and low, a voice like ten thousand volts through my stomach, too quiet for Char to hear. The cinnamon smell of his juicy fruit gum, and under that, diesel and leather.

It only takes two hours to get back to Barcelona; engine purring and Char like a child, excited by the sunshine and the sights. Flash of freckles in the mirror as she peels off her t-shirt, knots herself back into her bikini. Nico's tanned hands on the steering wheel, knuckles brushing against my bare legs each time he changes gears. No fuss at all at border control or the tolls, just hard on the gas through Figueres, Girona, Granollers.

*

With Char upstairs in the bath, Nico kisses me in the kitchen. One hand in my hair again, pulling my head back, hard. Cock pressing against me while the kettle shrieks and headlamps from the cars outside slice the ceiling into stripes.

'Didn't think I'd get to see you again,' he tells me afterwards, one thumb tracing my cheekbones, eyelids, mouth. Pirate glint of gold teeth. And even though at the time I'd rolled my eyes at him serenading us with those old Spanish boleros—flamenco guitars and pure vocals swollen with loss and longing, burbling from the radio as we lay around like cats in the sunshine, stoned and shipwrecked in his sheets—now I'm drowning in exhaustion and emotions I don't even know how to name.

'Bésame mucho,' I say instead, shyer than I've ever been. That famous Mexican song. He chuckles and obeys, his mouth on mine until we hear Char overhead, padding about in her towel, skin dewy with steam, a trail of puddled prints from her bare feet.

Nico goes out that night. 'Bueno, chicas, te dejo a ella,' he says. Ladies, I'll leave you to it. Chucks us his spare keys, gold jangle of metal chiming on the coffee table. It's bittersweet, but after last time I get the impression he's decided not to get too entangled. Clever boy, I think, catching his smutty wink and lopsided smile and giving him a wave that's hard to keep casual, even though his panther hips in his too-tight jeans are making my mouth water.

Later, in bed; her sun-streaked hair damp on the pillow with the tea tree smell of Nico's shampoo. Char's fingers thread through mine. Delirious from sex and lack of sleep, our conversation about where we'll go next feels weird, like a dream. With the lights out, we're always more honest. I tell Char I want to go and see Marie Laveau, the voodoo queen of New Orleans; carve three crosses on her grave the way they do in books and films. Char says she still wants her all-American road trip. See the Grand Canyon. Roller derby in Texas. The woods where *The Blair Witch Project* was filmed.

Sleep's sneaking in, and for once she isn't fighting it. But I am, still, although I'm tired too. Because I don't want the night to end yet.

(Sirens on the street outside, but for maybe the first time ever, she doesn't even flinch. Says something about how safe she feels, in our doughy duvet nest.)

'Don't go to sleep, Chardonnay.'

She rolls over, curls against me, paws my fringe out of my eyes. Her bottom lip between her teeth and a look somewhere between affection and exasperation, even in the dark.

'C'mon, Brit. I'm fine. No symptoms of concussion, and it's been long enough now. You know I'm not gonna die on you, right?'

'Nah, it's not that,' I reply, and her bauble-blue eyes narrow, curious and uncertain.

'What is it, then?'

'This.' And I kiss her as hard and long as I can, until it's morning again and Nico comes home: drunk, key scrabbling in the door. I hear his singing and a clatter of pans. The smell of coffee and churros, and *bésame mucho* in a rich baritone, warbling down the hall.

DAVID TAIT

BIOGRAPHY

David Tait's debut collection *Self-Portrait with the Happiness* was shortlisted for the Fenton Aldeburgh First Collection Prize and received an Eric Gregory Award in 2014. Poems appear in *Ambit, Magma, The North, Poetry Review, The Rialto* and *The Forward Book of Poetry 2014*. He lives and works in Guangzhou, China. These poems are from a new pamphlet, provisionally titled 'Particulate Matter'.

The Epidemic

We are watching a film about the epidemic
when he asks what the black spots are
and why they appear and won't wash off
and why this doesn't ever happen in China.

I switch on the VPN and google 'China, lesion images'
then watch his eyes, swivelling between bath houses,
some recent footage from a clinic in Chengdu
and the cut-off AIDS villages of Henan province.

He turns off the VPN and searches 'China, lesion images'
then shows me the first video. A doctor is staring deep
into the camera, 'This disease is spread by foreigners
and homosexuals. Since opening the borders infection rates

have rocketed.' I only understand him after translation.
I listen again, to this man's lilting Beijing accent.
I stare into his reasonable, almost-kind eyes,
then jab the screen, which loads the next video.

SELF-PORTRAIT WITH CICADAS
AND HORNETS

It is sometimes enough to wake late, make coffee
and sit on the stern wooden bench we use as a sofa
where you use me, in turn, as a headrest, and I run
the fingers of my left hand along your buzzcut
and rest my right wrist on your heart, unsure
if the pulse I feel comes from my wrist or your heart
or a mix of the two, just as all summer the cicadas
and construction workers have battled to tear up the air.

I step out to the balcony and stare down at the market.
It's citrus season again, and villagers are unloading
a minibus of pomelos, mangosteens and small caged rabbits,
the kind with quick breath and cloudy eyes, that lie still.
And there sits the man selling six nests of hornets,
no one goes near him, but every day he's there,
his hornets reverberating against the sides of their nets
as he sits with his head in his hands.

THE NIGHT BUS

I wake in the night to find we're driving past
the famous UNESCO site, stone Buddhas glowing

among the ruined stupas, dogs eyes igniting
by the roadside. Only me and the driver awake

and nothing seems changed—the pagoda drifts past
on its rise as we take the long bend past my old school.

It must be ten years. We approach Don Po roundabout,
cruise past the all-night noodle stalls and I see the stages

being erected for the egg banana festival—
a week of dancing for a fruit!—and then up,

up over the river. I can hear crickets chatter
through the undergrowth and think of him, still here

on the far side of town, with a wife now, a child.
The last time I came he told her we were going to play snooker

and she looked at me knowing we wouldn't play snooker.
It must be ten years. The river under me shifts like a sinister figure.

I see the other bridge flicker at the far side of town, the moths
still clattering into every streetlamp and then we're over, slowing,

the driver announcing the stop. You stir from your dream and ask if I know
where we are. 'The middle of nowhere,' I say, and your eyes slowly close.

'Kamphaeng Phet?' calls the driver, 'Kamphaeng Phet?'
And the door shuts out the singing air.

JACKIE HAGAN

BIOGRAPHY

Jackie Hagan is a poet, theatre maker and comedian. Jackie runs a project called Seymour Writers, using creative writing to enhance the lives of isolated adults. She was brought up on broken biscuits by scouse hecklers and is currently touring her new show *Some People Have Too Many Legs* (backed by the NRTF and Contact Theatre). The show is about Summer 2014, when Jackie suddenly had her leg amputated, found her dad, and fell in love with a posho. You can find her online at jackiehagan.weebly.com and on Twitter @jackiehagan.

SOME PEOPLE HAVE TOO MANY LEGS

I hate hospitals. They're so beepy. It's like living inside a techno album that doesn't know how to dance. The nurses keep asking me to score the pain from one to ten. We don't have words for this sort of thing, never mind numbers. This sort of pain is meant to come in quick stabs that you understand. This is a whole new bit of the human condition I knew nothing about before today. It's like learning that there's a colour you had never seen before, but shite.

One of the doctors comes in with a face like a raised eyebrow and runs a device over my legs that detects your pulse. Or rather, detects no pulse.

Times passes. The walls ache. I fret, text, tweet, want my Dad. Start to feel woozy.

Do you know what? I don't know if it's the morphine but every time the doctor comes he has a different head. I'll never learn all their names; Dr Jones, Dr Smith, Dr Frankenstein! But I remember the advice my Dad told me when I was little: 'What do you do if you don't know something? You make it up.'

Hello Dr Dre!

Dr Who comes to explain what's going on, he talks a big paragraph of god-knows-what and I very clearly, as unslurringly as possible, tell him to make sense. He tells me there are clusters of blood clots and they don't know why. There are a few things they can do, none of them are nice but it's important to endure them because they might save my legs and my life.

Save my legs?

Save my life?

'Miss Hagan, if we do this blah-blah procedure, you might not die.'

I might not die?

Might NOT . . .

Might NOT die.

I might not die!
I might be immortal!
Well, I've always suspected.

[. . .]

Liverpool, 1980. The Dog and Gun is rammed, 28 years before the smoking ban and they're smoking like they know it's coming. This is the type of pub that does quality meat raffles. There's always a terrier lapping beer from an ashtray and you don't sit in that seat—that's old Tommy's seat.

There's a gang of lads because there's always a gang of lads. One of them, a dirty blonde with an Irish twang, wears a green jumper and tries to be taller. He's seventeen. For the past fifteen minutes he's been trying to make eyes at The Girl. This pub is full of girls—girls with long brown hair and outfits they think the boys will like, but this girl is unapologetically her. She's 15 but she knows a thing or two, an enthusiastic name on the nightclub scene—one night she's a mod, the next night she's rocking but tonight she's a go-go dancer in silver boots and a black bobbed wig. She thinks she looks gorgeous. . . she looks drunk. She could be Jolene from the song. She could steal every girlfriend's boyfriend. She's not pretty, though, she's just something.

'Ey! Green jumper! I'm not willing to wait all night for yer,' she lies.

Before he knows it she's up in his face—her breath smells of Craven A Red and Sex on the Beach—his pulse quickens. She wants to tell him he has beautiful eyes, she wants romance and something gentle, but instead she shouts in her quietest foghorn scouse: 'I like yer jumper! Green!' 'Yes,' he says, several decibels lower. Her knees melt; he's quiet.

She drags him outside, the shock of cold; she pulls his arms around her and whispers, truthfully, 'I've chosen you.'

'Ey! Moira! Come 'ead—we're all going Midnight Mass!' the girl's best friend hollers. But Green Jumper and Silver Boots don't make it inside the church.

Nine months later, I'm born.

My Dad's protestant family thought themselves a little bit well-to-do so, when he brought home a fifteen-year-old, catholic, pregnant go-go dancer, all hell broke loose. But, for all the reasons my Dad's parents hated my Mum, he adored her. The waiting list for a council flat in them days was a long as the Mersey Tunnel so they were living in my Dad's teenage bedroom, as my Mum got bigger and bigger and more and more unwelcome in the house. But then something miraculous happened: Liverpool decided to build a promised land called Skelmersdale.

Skelmersdale! A new town with a bench and a lamppost!
Skelmersdale! Loads of cheap housing no one else wants to live in!
Skelmersdale! Skem.

It might have been a shotgun wedding but in the photos they've only got eyes for each other. Her in her white mini skirt and him in his penny collar. If you're a good catholic you're meant to name your baby after a saint, so they named me after one of Charlie's Angels.

Skem.

My Mum sits at the dining room table all day with loads of tiny pieces of shammy leather. She sticks them together to make one big shammy leather for 12p a go but in her head, she's dancing on a podium. The house reeks of superglue and hard graft. No one has a car, so the 16 miles between Skem and Liverpool gets further by the day. My Mum needs her mum; they write to each other. 'Not enough,' Mum says. My Dad gets a job far away, at the weekends I count the cuts on his hands. I make him little presents, like, I don't like the nuts ones in Revels so I suck the chocolate off and at the weekend I present him with a proud little pile of peanuts.

When I grew up I wanted to be posh—I wanted to live in a house that didn't smell of glue, so I had a plan. I would be clever and find my way out. When I grew up I would be a duck trailer. A duck trailer is someone who follows a duck's footprints in the snow and finds him at the other end. Duck trailers do not exist.

The thing about being a kid was this—I had this enormous sense of safety. It meant that everything was all right, even when it wasn't. Maybe if I eat enough Kinder Eggs I can get that back?

[...]

The thing about being sick is this—you get loads of attention, I love it. I'm getting a gazillion visitors a day and they all bring sweets, I currently have eight copies of the same issue of *Take a Break*.

My friends have decorated the wall next to my bed with get well cards and the best headlines cut out from the worst magazines—'A ghost sat my Geography A Level', 'My toddler has a spray tan' and 'I hide biscuits under my giant boobs'. Above my head is 'My dog walks sideways like a crab'.

I've made friends with the woman in the next bed—her name's Edna, she looks like a threadbare tennis ball with eyes, she's 72 and she hates scousers, mancs, lettuce, tea, toddlers, anecdotes, my tattoos, my hair, my face me and above all, nurses. I love Edna. I can imagine her in leather—she's got balls, she's a lone wolf, independent and narky. Edna is punk. Maybe I could be Edna?

On the other side is Sally. Sally likes jam, her eyes are wide and bewildered like a cow, she lies on her side. 'Nurse! Nurse! Nurse!' the nurses ignore her and this pisses me off, so I flop over and ask what she wants. She wants me to tickle her back. It is big and wet and the temperature of rice pudding just at the point the skin forms. Once I've done it she asks me to do it again. I tickle her big expanse of a back six times, then I start ignoring her too.

[...]

When I was three I got obsessed with doing the raindance. 'Ah!ah!ah!ah!ah!ah!' My mum told me that there is a sundance too—it's exactly the same, only silent.

When I was four I got obsessed with Brookside and my mum took me to the street where it is filmed. One drunken Christmas 14 years later I found out that she hadn't taken me to Brookside. She had just taken me to a cul de sac and pointed at it and called it Brookside.

When I was five my first hamster Bruce died and I asked my mum, is this going to happen to me? Am I going to die? And she said, 'No.' She said my entire family are immortal cos we've been chosen specifically by Paul Daniels.

Mums have to lie. It's in the job description between not going on rollercoasters and being capable of having a nervous breakdown while still cooking the Sunday roast. My parents were really ordinary but sort of bonkers through having kids too soon, too poor and too Skem. Then it filtered down to me, but in me it's worse because I've got this thing wrong with my eyes. It's honestly called Fuch's syndrome. Recently I was on a coach and the moon was incredible. I got everyone to look through the window at it, and then I realised, it was a clock on the side of a church.

When I was about 17 and I had this group of mates—you know the kind of mates who all hate each other? I was like the little daft mascot, the one who said the weird stuff and didn't quite fit in, I was Phoebe in Friends but less respected. We were in a park being teenagers when

I saw a beautiful seashell on the grass, the type you hold to your ear and hear the sea. I was made up, shouting the others over to look— and, as they got there, I realised that it was a beautiful seashell at all, it was a pile of vomit.

I went home that night and made a decision to stop. I would break the chain. I put all my teddies and childhood stuff in a bin bag, No more childish imagination and optimism, no more duck trailing. Duck trailing is stupid. The ducks can look after themselves.

*

I went down to the operating theatre. I had to lie flat on a metal table and keep very still. They were trying to get rid of the blood clots with lasers. I bit through my tongue with the pain, my mouth filled with blood, it tasted like steel. I wanted to kick off, I wanted my Dad to come and rescue me but I know he couldn't.

I had to cope, so I made a decision. I decided that I would make this experience, all of it, into an opportunity; this is my chance to grow up.

[...]

But . . . I don't want to do it! I want to be small and looked after. I don't have any resources. All I have is childish optimism and an ability to gab through the pain.

When I start to lose myself, usually in the night, I pretend that it's 1987 and I'm cuddled up on the couch with my Dad watching 'Allo 'Allo. 'Allo 'Allo was my favourite programme when I was seven—I thought it was just a bunch of nice people running a cafe, I didn't notice the war. How can you not notice the war? Me and my Dad were best mates back then, but then I kept getting older, I couldn't stop it; I started wearing lipstick and shouting. Then I went away to university.

71

In Skem everyone is pretty much the same as each other. So when I went to uni it was weird finding out that loads of other people live so different from me. I had never noticed that I was working class; it had just never come up in conversation. I got a bit sad and angry because I wanted my Mum and Dad to have nice things and a nice house, no bailiffs and no stress. I decided to work hard and get rich and send them both on holiday together. They'd never been abroad; I'd send them to Rome. I thought about sending them to Paris but that feels a bit too romantic, like admitting that your Mum and Dad have it off. Urgh.

And then, without warning, my Dad got sick and vulnerable like Dads don't. His foot went wrong. I went home and saw him cry for the first time, from the pain. I didn't like it, so I looked the other way. I went back to uni and concentrated on making friends and drinking. I got so good at the latter that I didn't really care about the former. I didn't go to see him again after that.

He got sick and then he had his foot off,
And then he had his leg off.
And then he had a stroke
And after that
he died.

Seems Paul Daniels was wrong.

I carried on looking the other way as hard as I could. It takes a lot of energy, constant distraction, it makes your back hurt, makes you sick.

Dr Suess comes, they have to amputate my foot.

I want my Dad to come with me to the operating theatre, but even if he could, there's still a door you go through where you're on your own.

[Blackout.]

And then it starts—my body isn't healing itself like it should, if the wound doesn't heal then they have to cut more off. Then if that doesn't heal they have to cut more off. Every three days the nurse shouts 'Dressing change!' and she pulls the curtains around and everyone has to leave and that's when I find out how bad it is. They also check my other leg, and my fingers.

Everyone is sombre around me. Well, they can piss off with that shit. I'm not a Faberge egg. I find out that if you're disabled you get called brave every five minutes, for anything! Like, for making plans with your life or eating a Twix, and you're meant to get offended because -to be fair - it's well patronising, I mean, the bravest things I've ever done are bugger all to do with disability. But, the thing is, I quite like compliments—so, after some consideration on the matter, I think my position is: 'How DARE you call me brave! But thanks for noticing, I am rather aren't I.'

Dressing Change: Wounds can progress both forwards and back through the phases depending upon intrinsic and extrinsic forces at work within the patient. It all depends on the colour of the tissue. Pink, good; grey, bad.

My Mum says she's got something to tell me. I'm terrified 'cos by now I think if anything goes wrong you amputate it. Turns out she stood in sick at the bus stop.

Dressing Change: I looked at it this time. My ankle is cut off on the diagonal, like the way you cut the stems of flowers.

I'm copying my Mum's coping methods. She says things like 'you live and learn', 'onwards and upward', 'you can only piss with the cock you've got'. She's uses clichés and she's nice. My English teacher used to say not to use the word nice. She said nice is lazy, but nice isn't lazy, sometimes nice is a lot of hard work. And I think clichés might get me through this.

Dressing Change: They didn't sugar coat it today. I don't want to be sat in a wheelchair all day staring into the middle distance. I'm good on my own, I'm gonna be a lone wolf, independent and narky. I'm going to be Edna.

I heard someone say once that you should never trust someone who hasn't been able to keep their own teeth . . . I haven't been able to keep both feet . . .

Dressing Change: Dr Spock tells me that there's only one thing they can do now. In order to clean the bacteria from the wound, they are going to put maggots on it. Real-life maggots with little wriggly bums! Dirty sods! And the maggots are coming from Wales. Wales?!? I can imagine them all sitting on a coach, with their little suitcases.

Edna disappears a lot, but that's what we do here—we disappear and we come back off our heads, or with bits missing, or we don't— but Edna just comes back the same, full of hatred and bile. I follow her and its turns out she's not going for tests or procedures, her husband is in the same hospital. I peep in and they're sat facing each other. I eavesdrop, which is easy cos she's shouting her minge off. It's the usual—the internet is evil, Starbucks is shit, the nurses are out to get her, and I wonder if she likes anything. Then she goes quiet, and she shouts: 'I LOVE YOU!', and then she starts crying, and then he holds her.

Dressing Change: Edna is not a lone wolf. Edna needs someone. I need someone. But who wants a girl with maggots on a stump?

There's no one here at night. In the midst of it all, I decide to open the box I nailed shut all those years ago. The box marked 'Dad'. I need him. He's the only other person who can understand what is happening to me. Plus everything is so bad that if I add some more bad then surely I'll hardly notice? What's the point in having a Diet Coke with take out, right?

I am a grown-up. A grown-up who needs her Dad. I gently turn to face him. I don't know if I've any memories. Maybe I killed the memories off because I was too scared to admit how much I had lost?

I concentrate. Remember Revels, him being sick, his foot going black; feel anger, like the sea closing in over the top of me, clenched; 'What do you do if you don't know something? Make it up!' and him crying, sick, *'Allo 'Allo* and lying on the couch, sadness makes my throat hurt, my heart goes too fast, can't bear the sickness, his face in pain, can't remember his smile, I close the box and nail it shut and decide I don't need to remember him.

I can do this on my own.

Dr Quinn Medicine Woman comes.
The Welsh maggots have let me down,
They've got to amputate my leg.

Blackout.

Fuchs syndrome! I've had a minor disability since I was born and that has never held me back—if anything that disability has made the world more beautiful!

Jarvis Cocker was a man in the '90s who was tall and thin and gangly and odd. He did not fit in. So, to cope with this, he wore shoes to make him taller, and clothes that made him ganglier, and acted odder. He became a sex symbol. That's when I learnt that if you have something about yourself you find embarrassing, if you try to cover it up it makes your body cringe, but if you make it a feature, if you make sure other people know that you are into your own gangliness, or your own asymmetrical face, or lisp, or you are into your own false leg, then it works. Eventually it becomes better than fitting in. It's certainly more fun. But how do you get to that point? 1) Pretend, fake it 'til you make it. 2) Throw some glitter on it, in whatever way you can. So that was my plan: when I get my false leg, I am gonna decorate it, I'm gonna be proud of it, I'm gonna make it a mascot of my resilience and my personality.

And then the drugs wore off and the pain came back. The same pain as before. Someone explained to me about phantom leg syndrome. The leg's gone but the pain stays. I ask how long it lasts for. It can last for the rest of your life.

It's not fair that my brain can remember pain in a leg that isn't there but it can't cope with remembering my Dad. I do not cope with this well. I totally and utterly lose my shit. Days, teenage talk, with the selfishness that comes from throwing in the towel, I make demands— no jokes—and make myself miserable. Everything is even more 'me' than usual. No glitter. Edna says I'm even more annoying like this. 'Someone turn her back on,' she says. 'She's going grey!'

My mum shows me a video on YouTube. Back home I have a reputation for really liking *The Wombles*, I collect old handmade ones from the '70s—only the really ugly and weird looking ones; I'm not interested in the normal ones. I have a womble outfit that I like to pretend is sexy (you can imagine how unsexy it actually is; I look like a desperate vole in a pinny). The YouTube video is from a show where all the people in the audience know me and know I'm in hospital, and the performer has got everyone on stage, and they all sing a song for me with some very good advice. 'Remember you're a womble.'

Indeed. I realise I'm being a little bit churlish. I realise that I know much more than I'm letting on. It's not just childish optimism and being able to gab through pain. I know loads. Dead important stuff, like 'Remember you're a womble.' Like, 'No one looks like Kate Moss, including Kate Moss.' 'The fight for sexual equality is not between men and women, it's between people and bellends.' 'If you're poor, you inherit anger; if you're rich, you inherit manners. And a house.' 'The minimum fill line on a kettle is real.' 'You live and learn, Jackie.' 'Jackie, you can only piss with the cock you've got.'

Maybe childish optimism isn't so bad. Being able to gab through the pain might be my new important life skill. I start writing certificates, just with biro on a bit of paper, congratulating anybody on anything that is good. I make one for a doctor who gives me more time than I know he has; one for a man for being really really Welsh. I congratulate people for having a symmetrical face, odd socks, and inappropriate eye contact, on having a head. I make Edna a certificate for coping well with hardship. Sshe laughs: 'You don't know the half of it, love.' She starts hanging out next my bed, I tell her I'm learning to be a better person. She teaches me how to iron using a shoe. I start to crave outdoors; I can smell it on people's skin when they come to visit. I decide I've had enough of other people looking after me. They won't let me leave the hospital, but I remember that I have another power—I was brought up by scousers, I have got a cob on, the gift of the gab, and I want out. On the way out, they give me a list of things to avoid; one of them is falling over.

As my Mum pushes me through the corridors I make a decision that I'm going to be strong, happy and really good at coping. I decide to see how long I can go without crying. No need for crying. I'm unflappable.

We get outside the hospital. I smell the sky—it's huge, it's so big they should call it 'outside'. Before we make it into the taxi I break down crying like a little kid. I'm small and I'm scared and my Mum understands.

I get to hers and on the floor there are little bits of paper, on each one is a duck footprint drawn in biro. I follow them and at the end is a duck with the words 'I love you'. If I'm gonna live my life then I'm gonna have to eat vegetables and do exercise and Wednesdays.

I don't think I'd be good at being a normal girl. I don't have brown hair and outfits I think the boys will like. I'm not pretty, I'm just, something... 'Unapologetically me'...

[Picks up puppets.]

I don't really know how to do love or life or learning to walk, I don't even know how to put a duvet cover on without getting stuck inside. But I remember what my Dad said. 'What do you do if you don't know something?'

Make it up.

[Holds up a Rainbow Brite doll, a little worse for wear. One leg has come off. Holds up a big teddy bear, a little worse for wear, in a Liverpool FC T-shirt. One leg has come off.]

Jackie: Dad, I've come to tell you something.

Dad: Ey you! You forgot about me for a bit didn't you! I'm all right up here. I've been having a pint with God.

Jackie: Don't be daft, you're not in heaven. You're in my head!

Dad: So you don't believe in God any more, eh? I remember the days you used to do your little prayers before you went to bed: 'Please lord can you make that lad from Take That come to my house and kiss me?'

Jackie: Shut up! His name is Mark Owen, actually.

Dad: Sorry, buggerlugs.

Jac: No, not 'sorry'. Don't say that. It's me who's sorry, I'm sorry I forgot about you for a decade. I thought it was easier to hide away than to live it. But both are hard aren't they.

['Allo 'Allo theme tune, quietly.]

Dad: Ey, softchops, I love you.

Jackie: I love you too. Dad,

Dad: Right, Shurrup now you, our programme is on:

[They watch telly together for a bit.]

Jackie: Dad? In 'Allo 'Allo, is there a war on?

Dad: Yeah, but it's allright love. We won.

[They watch telly for a bit.]

Dad: I'm proud of you, you know.

Jackie: Yeah, I'm proud of me too.

[She puts her head on his shoulder.]

JUDE ORLANDO ENJOLRAS

BIOGRAPHY

Jude Orlando Enjolras is a half Polish, Italian/British performance poet with a penchant for monsters and Shakespeare. He is a genderqueer polysexual trans boi, and political about it. *Poems for the Queer Revolution* is his pride and joy. 'The God Fearing Crack Dealers' Songbook,' from his novel-in-progress *Angels & Anarchists*, will appear in Dog Horn Publishing's forthcoming short fiction anthology *punkPunk!* Find him @LibrarianBoi and judeorlandoenjolras.wordpress.com.

THE SIEGE OF A LIFETIME

Once there were walls
Rising from bruised groin to bruised brain
To build temples to the old child god of cishet love

Once there were walls
Once upon a whole different world
Once upon a whole different world-build
A world of temples architected
Intelligently designed to keep love in
Rhetoric of sin snaking up the pillars with words
      like stone with words like stoning

Once there were walls
Festooned with grim gargoyles
Twisting temple arches into prison gates
Sending spires reaching down from the heavens
      and into a hell not fit for poetry

Once there was a graveyard of temples
With crypts walled like cubic enigmas
Every answer wrong
Every day judgment day
The sins of the flesh revisited on transgressing flesh
      like the lash of a conqueror's flag

I hid behind walls once
Waiting for a single raised brick to connect like a raised hand
      like a body too heavy

I felt the walls once
Pressing against me with the weight of the wrong clothes
All the while shedding weight to rise and be worthy
     of the dread god of my temples

I put up walls once
To bury the memory of violence disguised as love

I look at the walls now
The acropolis scattered at my feet
Stone eroded by the slow patient work of time
Stone scattered by hands scrabbling for salvation
     for a shred of sense for something

I have made my home among new walls these days
Weeds climbing up the side of cafés like castles
Dive bars my strongholds
Libraries my battlements

I have made new walls to stand against the tyranny of the old
Waging war for my right to grief and identity
It is the siege of a lifetime

I have made new walls with these two hands
Raised from the old not like phoenixes from ashes
     but like damned dead redeemed.

'CATCH YOU LATER, YOU ANGEL-HEADED HIPSTER'

Says the anarchist-a-like on the Bakerloo train headed north
Now you listen here lad, I think to myself
I had the hair of angels before it was cool
Or did I
Or are they
Angels, I mean
The Catholic cherubs that haunted my nightmares
From frightfully nice frescoes and terrifying children's Bibles
They wouldn't want to know me now
And the martial archangelic host
Would hardly admire the armour forged against the anvil of my anger
There is a languor
To the music of my spheres
Oiled by home-brewed beer
I have more in common with the beast under Michael's boot
Than with the so-called angel doing the trampling
I'm only just now sampling life and lust
After a life in death in heaven
I knew I was right as a child reading up on eternal salvation
As conjured up by a compatriot and colleague, ca. 1300 AD
I never made it past purgatory
Up to dull-as-ditchwater heaven
There's one hell of a party down here
And I am just about done living in fear
All my life I have denied my own voice
But tonight
I will raise it
Soaring beyond the underworld
As I sing the songs of my people
Demons and dragons and devils
In silk and lace and rubber and plaid
Goth punk dandies fallen through the cracks of respectable London
Angel wings beautifully burnished with the fury of free will.

TEAM FREE WILL 4EVA

I'm pretty sure I was born this way, this trans I mean, but for the sake
of argument—your argument, just so we're clear; I take no pleasure
in debates over my existence like I'm stuck in an eternal recurrence of
undergrad philosophy—for the sake of argument

Let's say I chose this
Let's say I chose to be a boy because being a girl hurts
Let's say I chose to be a handsome boy rather than the girl who no one
wants, or wants all wrong
Let's say I chose to be a boy who likes boys rather than the girl who
lives in fear and is taught—educated—reminded to call it love, or else
Let's say I chose to be a poet boy rather than a sliver of a shadow of a
novelist, as scared to put word on paper as she is to put on a kilo or
the wrong dress
Let's say I chose to be a boy because my girlhood's been shattered and
slashed and torn time after so many bloody times that the pieces no
longer fit, glue consumed by blood not bloody metaphorical
Let's say I chose to be a boy because being a girl hurts
Let's say I chose this

Your point is?

Choice is good
Agency and consent too
I want to choose my own adventure
And neither man nor God is going to tell me what to write.

FAIRYTALE OF THE WRONG BIT OF LONDON

4am hits
Or some such
Small hours all look the same
As they stretch into frightful infinity
Dysphoria reaches into my brain like the roots of rotten fairytales
All fairytales nightmares full of mirrors, mirrors full of lies
I toss and turn in your arms
Night terrors as bright as any God-given day
I reach up to my head
Nails poised to prise dysphoria from my temples
I look at you and I ask
'Are you sure that I'm really a boy?'
Hoping not expecting you to keep me sane
And then somehow
Somewhere in your twenty years
You find wisdom enough to say that
I am a boy, and I look it
I am a boy, and I walk it
I must be a boy
Or else how would I turn you on?
And with that
That earnest lust wrapped in a whole lot of love
You wrap me in your arms, tighter than before
And just like that
You turn my dysphoria off like a switch
Just then
The darkness seemed like too much to handle
But right now
Right here in your arms
I feel braver than I have in a long time

I think I'll sleep with lights off tonight.

MITCH KELLAWAY

BIOGRAPHY

Mitch Kellaway is a queer transgender writer, an independent researcher, and the co-editor of *Manning Up: Transsexual Men on Finding Brotherhood, Family & Themselves*, an anthology of personal narratives by trans men. He serves as Assistant Editor for Transgress Press and has written for the *Huffington Post*, *PolicyMic*, and *Original Plumbing*. His creative writing has been published in numerous literary journals and queer and trans* anthologies.

He is from Boston, MA.

Muscle Memory

There's an odd lull between the bursts of energy needed to set up an empty dining room and to serve dinner for an unrelenting six hours. While the hands are preoccupied with wiping grime off ketchup bottles or half-shearing straws of their paper wrappers, while the adrenaline is ramping up to meet the hungry hordes any minute now but not quite yet, my coworkers and I can be found half-asleep, sending surreptitious text messages, or gleefully dropping bombshells of personal information on each other. We perfect slumbering while wide-eyed, hunching to hide glowing cell phones, and shrugging like what? Nah, it was no big deal.

If the gossip is boring, we move on to the next person; if it's awkward, we can always scatter to our busywork. But if it's juicy, two or three of us—select newsmill royalty, since we'd lose our jobs if we all relaxed at once—will march out back for a smoke break. The stories will filter among the rest of the staff throughout the shift: breakups and hookups and ragers and benders passed server-to-busser-to-bartender along with piles of dirty dishes, beers, and smoked racks of ribs. Revealing ourselves in rushed, nonchalant tidbits sustains us in a way that fulfilling strangers' barbecue cravings cannot. It keeps us coming back, even when the tips are shitty.

Over the past year I've been working at Meat-N-Three, I've gotten used to this place's pulse, so different from college. Its ebbs and flows structure my everyday: from how I eat and sleep, to how I socialize and decompress, to how I reveal and process my ups-and-downs. It's not a stretch to say that this restaurant has become my life; working overtime and on a schedule at odds to my 9-to-5 peers, most of my feelings of productivity and belonging are centered here. Meat-N-Three gives me meaning.

At first, though, I had to consciously resist the mainstream stance towards service: that it holds inherently less value than other work. There's an unspoken assumption that in the arc of a lifetime, the four or five years I'll spend slinging comfort food and margaritas and, later on, lattes and croissants, will be nothing more than a way to pay the bills on my path towards my real 'life's work'. This is not, of course, a script handed to the undocumented, undereducated, perpetually stoned, or single parents among us—just to the half of the staff who are earning degrees on the side of earning gratuities.

But given just the reality in front of me, grease stains, sweat, and fatigue prove, thankfully, to be great equalizers. When I'm laboring with fifteen others to turn two hundred tables a night, my 'A' in Intro to Women's Studies pales in comparison to my ability to hold four steaming plates at once. After months of practice, I can perform this feat while simultaneously talking shop with the food runner and keeping my eye on whether the dish bins or trash need to be changed. When my section's full, when I'm delivering appetizers and drinks as quickly as they can be ordered, and when my coworkers are equally occupied, I hit a kind of flow state. We work together as parts of a well-oiled machine, updating each other on ongoing shifts in clipped exchanges: 'The pilsner just kicked,' 'The host is combining our tables into an eight-top,' 'We're out of pecan pie,' 'Table four wants to break a fifty.'

On unusually slow nights, we'll commiserate about this phenomenon after, yet again, one of us types in a wrong order or forgets to fetch a customer's cornbread. The more frenzied the pace and the more tasks that need to be juggled, the better we all are at our jobs and the more able to take unexpected changes in stride. Restaurant life has a logic and rhythm all its own.

*

I'd sat on coming out as transgender for seven years. Whenever the desire had bubbled up to the surface, it had never seemed like quite the right time to do it. I was sure, somehow and someday, that I'd fit it into my schedule, but with my college course load and extracurriculars, I just couldn't imagine diverting my time and energy right now. Then, laid low by a bout of depression, I suddenly had plenty of time on my hands. I'd failed a class and, faced with knowing that I'd probably do it again if I didn't address my heavy heart, I took a leave-of-absence.

The funny thing about having three-quarters of a college degree is that, at least in an urban center saturated with 'higher' education, it doesn't get you any further in the job market than if you hadn't bothered pursuing three years of $150,000 in classes. When I walk into Meat-N-Three, I enter at the bottom rung: taking phone orders. In this world, experience reigns supreme. Bruises, muscles, gritted teeth, emotional shutoff, smoker's hack, burned forearms, irredeemably dirtied shirts. I embrace the departure from the world of formal education, where status is accrued half through how long you can sit thinking, half through who you know.

Though I've spent time working as a dorm cleaner, I lack the experience of toiling to earn a living, of spending most of my energy making sure I've garnered enough money to keep myself going. The minute I leave college I feel my safety net fall away. With no university-provided health insurance, housing, or meals, sinking or swimming falls squarely on my ability to find and maintain a job, and my undisciplined body's ability to remain healthy and able. I take the first apartment and position that come my way; I learn how to work a stove, read a bus schedule, budget for groceries and write a check. I'm somewhat mortified that I don't know how to do such things already. It's all, in a word, draining.

Until it's not. I can't pinpoint the moment that everything became muscle memory, but somewhere near the end of my first year as a working stiff, I barely have to think about how to perform given tasks. This both goes for duties at home and at work, where I've come to spend most of my time. I'd been promoted to a server after about a year of answering phones, and night after night of looping the same dining room—gathering orders and dirtied plates, stopping at the service station for silverware and cornbread, and grabbing waters or drink tickets from the bar on the way back to my tables—had become pleasantly automatic. My robot body goes to work trading pulled pork for tips, and my mind is free to think on other matters. Mostly they involve how much I can devour on my break or if I feel like joining others after work at our go-to bar or about the latest installments in budding workplace friendships.

But sometimes my attention is rudely drawn back to the fact that I am embodied. I hear my voice pitch particularly high trying to please a customer; a well-placed grease stain draws my attention to my breasts or hips; my cargo shorts, stuffed with receipt books and pens, sag precariously low, threatening commentary from whoever

90

feels invited to look at my boxers. Of course, as a server I've learned to constantly 're-set': with information and stimuli flying from all directions, remaining steady is a matter of pausing to absorb impact, taking a deep breath, then trudging forward as planned. But I have a particularly difficult time zoning out the instances I'm made aware that not only do I inhabit a female form, but that it is a social body destined to engage in a hundred interactions a night.

'Hey, sweetheart,' I'll get at least once weekly from some middle-aged white man, surrounded by his slightly embarrassed family, his voice thick with a townie accent. His performance of man-being-served relies on calling out our gender distinction, and my role as waitstaff compels me to nod in approval. This, apparently, is the cue for him to ask my name and I always give it, though I dread it being used excessively for the next hour he's here dining. Each time he enunciates the syllables through a smarmy smile, I feel simultaneously enraged and paralyzed—this is simply not the place to express my disgust with needlessly gendered conventions. How could I even explain to this man that the behavior he justifies as (genuinely believes is?) 'polite' is laden with a history of destructive gender hierarchy?

I'm convinced that none of my female coworker likes this kind of patronizing exchange either, but I doubt it also ignites my own underlying fire: I don't just want these men to know that I'm not a willing co-star in their script, but that I'm not that name or that gender at all.

*

A few months into serving full-time, I tabulate my expenses and realize that I can cover them with only a half-month of labor. Rather than take this as reason to lighten my load, I begin picking up extra work, often pulling 'oubles'—back-to-back shifts in the same day. It's thrilling that I have two weeks a month to earn as much extra income as possible to do whatever I want with. It's an entirely new feeling, being able to afford indulgences I hadn't let myself fully dream about having until now.

Mostly I spring for flashy hightop sneakers; when I reach a

number in excess of what I can practically use, I rationalize buying new colors by matching my entire outfit each day. Then I realize I haven't replaced my t-shirt selection since I left home for college. As I gradually renew my wardrobe, I recognize, tritely enough, that I'm emerging into a newer, more adult me. I reach my pinnacle of self-gratification by doing something I'd always wanted: stepping into a barbershop.

As the barber pumps his hydraulic chair, raising my 5'2" butch body to meet his clippers, I know I'm going to receive exactly the kind of haircut I've desired. Though the salons I've visited have tried valiantly with scissors, they could only approximate the tightly cropped fade reflected back at me when he's done. Last-minute I decide to throw in a flourish, and ask for racing stripes; his grip is both firm and gentle as he carves them with a straight razor, two deep ridges exposing my scalp. I step down and walk to the register, pulling out a wallet bristling with twenties. I pluck one out and hand it to him, feeling downright royal as I tell him to keep the change.

New outfit, new kicks, new trim—I've done so much to actualize an exterior that mirrors my interior, it's just too damn bad I can't simply walk down the street to buy the beard, flat chest, and baritone I yearn for. I know transition's not that easy, yet as with so much in life, this too comes down, at least in part, to money. Of course, to say that my new discretionary income was the catalyst for actualizing my manhood wouldn't be wholly accurate; like any complex achievement, it required a number of ideal conditions. Without the backdrop of a stable job, apartment, and relationship, medical transition would not have been possible, particularly for someone who requires a modicum of predictability before engaging with the unknown.

But I may have found reason to continue foregoing transition indefinitely—in the same way I now put off buying a needed, though pricy, asthma inhaler—had I not suddenly, unavoidably been able to afford it. Anyone who knows what it means to 'get by' rather than thrive, to scrimp rather than satiate, to prioritize rather than splurge knows what it's like to make do with a gender that doesn't quite fit. You find ways to cope and overlook—and though what you lack adds pounds of resistance as you march forward, you continue to do so.

Not being a man didn't mean I lived an unhappy life; I experienced much joy and success in my female incarnation. It meant I didn't live a full life, with so much of my energy needlessly spent on quieting the anxious, dysphoric undercurrent especially present throughout social interactions. The experience gives me little doubt that the day this world sees a fairer distribution of wealth, it will also see many more folks, liberated from the burden of medical expenses, transition their genders.

*

In a sense, my transition actually does start with a simple walk down the street. Working in the commercial hub of my just-outside-the-big-city town means almost everything I need is within a three-block radius. Now able to afford $100 therapy appointments out-of-pocket, I begin seeing a therapist five minutes from Meat-N-Three. Entering his office, I tell myself this is simply to process the depression that had forced me out of school; by the end of our first session, I've admitted that I'm there to finally start talking transition. This means waiting at least three-to-six months for my therapist to hand over a letter clearing me for testosterone use—though I know this requirement is becoming less strict as time passes. The next day I decide on a name from the few I've been contemplating and fill out the paperwork at Probate Court.

Though I know it'll be at least a couple months before my name change is official, and probably a half-year before my voice starts cracking, I can't help but announce my transition at Meat-N-Three. I'm definitely in for some clumsy interactions as the news transfers unevenly throughout my seventy coworkers, but it's hard to fathom being misnamed over a hundred times a night as we all pass bumper car apologies, status updates, and stingy-tipper warnings. Besides, I feel like a child with a new toy: I can't help but proffer it to everyone I know, shiny and worthy of admiration.

The next day I swing behind Meat-N-Three and seize upon the first coworker I find: a new hire straight from high school. She's dreamily puffing on a cigarette, her perfect bleached hair looking awkward stuffed into the required baseball cap. We barely know each other, so we share a standard greeting.

'Hey, what's up?' she asks, neither interested nor uninterested.

'I legally changed my name to Mitchell,' I answer, grinning.

'Oh yeah?' She looks up from her reverie.

'I'm transitioning to male,' I add.

'Oh yeah?' she repeats. We blink at each other. 'Good for you.'

'Thanks,' I reply, and she sinks back into her heavy-lidded contemplations. This is exactly what I needed: for my transition to be a blip on someone's radar, duly acknowledged as it's announced, but layered between the other blinking dots, a shift taken into account with all the others. Undoubtedly, its meanings will be hashed and rehashed during lulls, each coworker making sense of my transition and comparing notes. I purposefully don't give them much background or detail: I relish the thought that they'll all have to process without the aid of a neat, tell-all narrative.

Walking into the restaurant each day, we've learned to expect a reality slightly different than the day before. Lily got fired! The computer is down until 4pm! Call that guy "Mitch"! We're out of hushpuppies! We adapt immediately and without comment, making the needed adjustments to get through the shift as smoothly as possible. My name and pronoun changes are much the same, and experience a range of adeptness from newbies to the old-hands. It's messy and it's wonderful, the outpouring of back slaps and admiring nods, the brilliant teachable moments and apologetic fumbles.

There's something delightfully queer about asking someone to look at me—with my same smooth cheeks, high voice, and curvy hips—and ask, without elaboration or warning, for them to call me 'he'. In order to do so, they have to ask themselves some questions—is this okay? Why? Why not?—and whether or not I'd like the unspoken answers, the social pressure—everyone else is doing it!—inevitably leads them to acknowledge my manhood, though some never quite catch on to the pronoun switch. Even then, they experience a queering of language as their discomfort forces them to think up new ways to avoid gendered wording. I soon decide to leave Meat-N-Three for another job opportunity before I ever sprout a whisker, and by that time I am Mitch to everyone; it's become automatic. Muscle memory.

This makes it easier to face the Hey-Sweethearts of our small world. During one of my final shifts, a perfect specimen is seated at one of my tables, his extended family spread out banquet-style throughout my entire section. The patriarch, ever chivalrous, waits to be the last served.

'Hey sweetheart,' he begins, 'what's your name?'

'Mitch,' I respond and look him straight in the eye.

'What was that?' he returns, bewildered.

'Mitch.'

'I'm not going to call you that,' he replies with the shake of his head. Readying myself to walk away and fume in private, his wife cuts in quietly.

'Honey, it's not what you think. It's Mitch, not Bitch.'

'Oh, Mitch!' he responds, a little too loud and too cheerfully. We share an uneasy laugh and I turn away quickly to fill their drink orders, smiling to myself. Neither name has allowed him to settle into his practiced, ego-puffing exchange. Bitch—too honest, too close to the role he assigned me on sight. Mitch—too queer, too close to his own once familiar territory.

SPARK

Watching video blog after video blog made by men who look like me—all betraying, at least, the seemingly eternal pubescence of my own trans early adulthood—I come to a revelation. These guys are all measuring themselves by other men, seeking male and masculine-of-center company and validation; even the ones who are proudly feminine and openly transgender rarely mention occasions where they interact with trans women. And when I think about it, neither do I. The wrongness of it strikes me hard, cutting through the fog of a mind stuck too long in "researcher" mode.

That night, I'm bursting to share my discovery over dinner. 'These trans men think they have more in common with cis men than they do with trans women,' I announce to my butch lesbian friend Sandy. We're revealing the gems we'd mined from our semesters' research projects—mine an undergrad in gender studies and hers a master's in social work. 'Obviously,' is her glib response. She sips her beer and flashes that easy smile that always invites me to agree. Nonetheless, I'm taken aback, suddenly aware that I've queitly held onto the belief (the hope?) that people who transgress gender lines have more mutual—deep, intimate, unspoken, primal—understandings than those who share male or female embodiment, regardless of gender history.

Why wasn't it obvious to me that young trans men would move towards a common ground of maleness and away from a common ground of trans-ness? Is that what I'm unconsciously doing too?

To be honest, I'd chosen my semester's research subjects—trans male YouTube video bloggers—because I knew I could relate to them, because their amateur self-documentaries had nourished my own nascent trans-ness when that was critical for me. Moreover, I was a sure feminist before I was a sure man: I knew I had no place speaking for women. Early background research only confirmed my approach: many trans women were vocally, and understandably, opposed to becoming academic pawns, trotted out and prodded for someone else's benefit. Being a trans researcher gave me no privileged access.

Yet I've always been drawn to the soft company of women; as a feminist, I've always been drawn to women's advocacy. This was the case both before and after I transitioned to male, though the transition made it easier to see where I stood within it all—no longer did I have to wonder if my joy in sharing space had to do with also sharing a gender. And I had only to think of the numerous occasions I'd given cisgender men a wide berth, most recently the one who grinned deliriously at me as we stood side-by-side at a busstop, and whispered 'faggot' over and over as I boarded the vehicle. He'd held my eyes tauntingly as the bus lurched forward and I couldn't help but turn to peer backwards out the window as I retreated.

I take a swig of my beer and look back at my good friend, look up at the kind face that towers a good foot above my own tiny frame. She's a cis woman possessing her own masculinity; soft curves in a six-foot frame, warm and reassuring like a bearhug. I recall that she and I are supposed to be at odds on the battlefield of gender expression, but the term 'FTM-Butch Border War' sounds like an alien land of yore. How is it that the gravitational pull of my beard and low-voice should hold her masculinity in deferential orbit? That when standing side-by-side we are supposedly read in comparison, rendering her unalterably more feminine—shorthand, in patriarchal societies, for 'lesser than'? Masculinity has more than enough space to spare, at least where I'm looking from the queer side of life.

Anyway, Sandy and I know without speaking that in reality, right here and right now in our present generation, that she and I are two different sides of the same coin; two keys sung for the same tune. It's made me start to itch: the way I feel echoed and buoyed in the presence of Sandy's masculinity is how I desire to feel in the presence of a woman's trans-ness, and how I hope to make her feel too.

*

The next week, I snap a silly picture of my wife and I embracing as we descend the escalator to the subway. I pass it to her, as usual, to deem it treasure or trash, but she quickly returns my phone with a pensive look. Our photo has been background 'bombed' by the female figure looming behind us. The angle renders the light around her blonde wig a halo; her averted gaze and tight-lipped expression make her appear as if she's anxiously leaving the frame.

She—the unknown transgender woman I notice weekly on the bus to work—haunts the image, both a part of my world and yet held apart. I immediately delete the candid, making sure her nonconsensual presence will not be carried with me beyond the station. But I cannot tap the glowing red wastebasket icon without hesitation—erasure feels callous. In a parallel world, we are kin.

Stepping onto the bus mid-route, I can often count on spotting her: visibly white and middle-aged, dressed in a flowy top over jeans and sensible sneakers, her face sporting a light layer of blush. Whenever I see her, I instantly think family. Though I'm half her age and her eyes look straight through me, I once more imagine that a shared history of trans-ness would link us—but only if we could acknowledge it. I just want to sit beside her, shake her hand, hear her voice and see if her eyes have crows-feet when she smiles. Instead, I do her the favor of passing by, the honor of not reading her as anything but the cisgender default.

I instinctively assume that any recognition between us would constitute a threat—to her, that is, and not to me—because we inhabit a system in which my male gender is placed hierarchically above her female one, in which my 'passability' is placed hierarchically above her visibility, and in which my masculinity, no matter how effete, lends me armor if my right to be here were ever questioned. Our interaction would inevitably be another instance of a man assuming access to a woman's space, and I just can't be a party to that social project. So I hold my peace and keep my trans-ness to myself, presuming she would think it better that she keep her own trans-ness to herself.

How would I even send her the subtle message that I'm safe when she has every reason to assume I'm not? How would I even introduce myself if our circumstances, our entire world, were different? If being clocked as transgender were not a let-down, a failure, a second-best?

Still, part of me wonders if she wants her lived experience acknowledged anyways, so that neither one of us would be so alone in the self-contained in-between of our commutes. I inevitably split the difference by catching her eye and smiling, trying to beam warmth from my eyeballs. She looks away. Did I just imagine that faintest spark of recognition?

MY TWO

i.
couple kelloid
half moons
pectoral rims
i'm told
they beg
concealment
angry pink &
slightly jagged
they would
reveal
to knowing
lookers
too much
of my
(body)
history—
that I took
what
parts I needed
& shed the
rest
abandoning tissue
like
a sculptor's
excess stone

ii.
slashes—
my two
don't won't
portend
injury nor
disease, too
unrandom
for
an accident
a symmetry
too crafted
cannot will not
be residue
of emergency
look!
away | closer
they lie
emblazoned
but never
whisper come probe
my wired flesh
my wounds warmed over
my made-to-clash
my subterranean

ENDNOTE

'Look!' inspired by Jamison Green, '"Look! No Don't!" The Visibility Dilemma for Transsexual Men' in Kate More and Stephen Whittle (eds), *Reclaiming Genders: Transsexual Grammars at the Fin de Siecle*, (New York: Cassell, 1999).

BORN

'born this way' is
only
the brief second after
womb exit
next moment, we're
shifting constantly our
raw material:
forms, minds, spirits, our
shared human birthright:
one meat lump
heaving with
blood & air.
this: enough without
being stretched taut,
we imperfect canvases
for sacred cores,
we floating blips confounded
by watchful constellations
of iris light & pupil dark.

TOOK THAT

six years ago two women
took that hollow bank
frame kept, insides gutted
each daybreak a
hulking presence fades,
drips espresso

enter warm, voice floating
gelled in extra air
upwards then, atom-thin
gray filigree for a
fortress-high ceiling

& that brute money vault
now a heavy jaw stuck open
its teeth painted flowers
and countertops--lids drooping
low as three-year-old eyes

Tara Ali Din

Biography

She's British, she's Muslim and she's bisexual. And before you ask, yes it is possible, British Muslims are very common. Tara Ali Din's play *The Lesborrist Tapes* (written with Joshua Ferguson) was broadcast on Roundhouse Radio during LGBT History Month 2013, and has been performed either in whole or in part at Three Minute Theatre, Taurus and Edinburgh Fringe.

Tara is one of the original members of Young Enigma, and was one of our 2013 LGBT History Month Writers-in-Residence.

AN ACT OF TERRORISM

I'm about to perform an act of terrorism.

[Clicks on vibrator, then clicks it off.]

Lesbian terrorism.

There's nothing to be gained from blowing you up. Blowing you, well, that's another matter. Getting you people blown, getting you to explode in your pants, would certainly do a lot more to change your minds about how you live your disgusting, *decadent* Western lives.

[She rummages in her 'bomb' and digs out a pack of e-cigarettes.]

[She lights one and smokes it by turning upstage and lifting her veil briefly. Pause.]

I'm a safe terrorist—doctor said I have to take care of my lungs. *[takes a drag]*

I probably think too much about tits to be a really good terrorist. Do you know about the five pillars in Islam? One of the pillars is supposed to be getting to that box in Mecca, not into the box of the hottest waitress in the hookah bar.

[Thinks for a minute.]

[She turns sharply to the audience, as if automatically scolding them.]

That's a hookah as in for smoking, not for poking. Don't be filthy with it.

God! It's as hot as fucking Jahannam in this fucking thing.

[She takes off a burkha to reveal another burkha.]

Fuck me running, that is so much better. You know what, they say this whole get-up is to protect modesty, but that's only physical modesty. I mean, girls who are, like, rougher than the fiery cavity of a djinn's arsehole don't really need that kind of modesty, do they?

What about people like me? Or possibly you? Where being . . . really . . . really good at sex (or not having any complaints), really enjoying it, really hungering for it. You don't need a veil to hide that. It's hidden all the time. You don't even know it's there until you, as it were, Terry's Chocolate Orange. You know, tap and unwrap.

So we have this little secret, this little burkha worn not on the outside, but in your fucking soul, at the core of your sexual being. I think everyone wears it to a certain extent. Maybe you're not as covered as you might be, but you certainly wear it. And . . . Oh God, inshallah, I will tear that enforced modesty off the souls of everyone in the world.

[Suddenly starts reciting Urdu with great reverence. She is, in fact, quoting choice lyrics from the song 'I Kissed A Girl' by Katy Perry.]

[After prayer, take off emergency burkha.]

But you know, we all have our own prayers, our own devotions and shows of penitence. There's a certain bent appeal in abandoning all of one's previously held beliefs in order to truly, properly follow one's heart, but I just can't seem to do it. All I find is that who I am perverts what I believe. Never the other way around. And showing my wrists and ankles to people in public doesn't inflame them nearly as much as I had been given to understand.

I felt a little bit cheated when I found out that sex isn't the great and terrible surrender to temptation, the unholy euphoric rush of pleasure and devilish abandon that I thought it would be. I imagine you did as well. Maybe it was just barely a minute's worth of febrile hip-thrusts ending in stickiness, blood and shame? Maybe it was just boring. Perhaps Allah, in His great ineffable wisdom, made your first time like that so you'd think 'bugger this for a lark' and head straight back to your life of penitence and devotion, just hoping that the rush you felt at the time of the Call to Prayer would be better than any orgasm.

I guess that all depends where your call to prayer is.

[Pause.]

Is it any wonder why we cry out what we do in the throes of sexual passion that borders on the spiritual? 'Oh God, oh fuck!' and so on.

As it says in the holy text of Islam, prayer is strengthened manifold when it is done in a group. I wonder if I could attest to the same being true of spiritual, sexual passion?

[Starts putting first burkha back on.]

Could there be a moment, when, en masse, a group of people devoted to a common cause, with their bare skin revealed to all, could bare their sexuality to each other in a way that causes the same rush as a prayer, as the Holy Mass, as a Sabbath prayer? Or the blessing of a newborn child, that which was brought about by animalistic rutting. The product of the union is holy and in the image of God, so why can't the process to create it be holy as well? Or is it that true holiness can only be brought about by perverted and unholy acts?

[Pause.]

Either way, there are some interesting conclusions to be drawn. And either way, I am following the calling deep, deep, deep within me by acting on it.

[Puts second burkha back on.]

ANDREW MCMILLAN

BIOGRAPHY

Andrew McMillan is a poet, facilitator and creative writing lecturer. One of the original members of Young Enigma, he was one of our 2013 LGBT History Month Writers-in-Residence. Andrew's first full-length collection *Physical* is due out in July 2015 from Jonathan Cape.

EDITOR'S NOTE

These poems were originally commissioned for LGBT History Month 2013, where they formed a literary tour of Manchester. You can follow the tour on Google Maps via youngenigma.com/progress.

PROGRESS

INTRODUCTION

When thinking what to call this commission, it seemed a disservice to simply call it a walk (you can do it from the comfort of your own home), a map (it will get you lost), a tour (implies something more purposeful), a survey (it is representative only of myself), an excursion (there is no end destination, it's cyclical) or a guide (it has no information within it that could really be of any profound use). I hooked upon the word progress. It seems somehow pertinent. Thinking not only of progression of LGBT rights, the progression of a city through gentrification and rebuilding but also of the idea of a royal progression, of the idea of going out amongst the people. Poetry is so often seen as being something 'other' to our ordinary lives, that it exists, almost like royalty, in closed off spaces only accessible to the very few. With this commission, I wanted poetry to walk around the city, I wanted it to go to unpoetic places and declare itself, I wanted to progress through a city in a poetic way.

As a model for this I used my great poetic hero Thom Gunn, who's later work focussed particularly on ordinary parts of San Francisco streets; I wanted to poeticise the mundane areas of Manchester in much the same way.

One final thing, this is a map of a city I don't live in any more. This is a map of a city I only lived in for a year. This is the map of a city I only lived in for a year and which I am already starting to forget. Places conflate with each other. People merge into other people into the same person into the same lover into the same memory. Other cities become Manchester; Manchester becomes other cities. This is not a factual guide to the LGBT scene of Manchester, although many such documents exist. This is not a memoir. This is a snapshot of how my brain mapped the terrain around it while I was living, for the first time in my life, in a city. Faced with something new, we will grasp for something which is familiar, and what can be more familiar than the human body—be it yours or someone else's. Familiar and yet unfamiliar. Unheimlich. Un-homely. A city which never asked for you and which you have no right to map. Except you do. Except we all do. Everytime we walk or run or drive or get a bus, we rewrite the city.

travel   transience   the coming and going of bodies   of people
of relationships   when I lived in Manchester I was working full-
time as a freelance writer, in Bournemouth, Newcastle, London,
Bristol, Weymouth; all over   I was always in the train station
oftentimes at dawn or midnight

it's a very lonely occupation   travelling alone is a very lonely
way to move   you begin to watch people   you begin to watch for
connections with people   falling in love is never as easy as when
you're on a train

WHAT MY BODY DID NEXT

the man   the train   the borrowed pen   the card to Christiana   the
beautiful boy asleep in his hair   *merry (late) Christmas* the
beautiful boy awake in his face   somewhere a choreographer is
forcing beauty from the human form   25km away someone is using
your fouryearago face to look for chat and friendship   *Christiana   I
am sorry   time is something the trains invented*
I remember none of the last 68 words you said to me

a poem from one moment   waking   after a night out   and having
the momentary struggle of locating onself   realising I could see
the bedroom window of the person I was trying to fall in love with
realising I didn't know where I was

again I think travel   leaving   departures   cities make you look
up   that's how they're built   the glass is so tall you have to look up
you have to look up and you're confronted with your all smallness
because you see the trails of planes tens of thousands of feet up flying
thousands of miles   there is nothing static in a city   everything is
fluid   everything is always shifting   people are always leaving

I HAVE THE FIRST TWO LINES OF A POEM

the missiles fly like storks
they go to roost in market stalls and people's roofs

love   if I'm conscripted I won't go
I'll bury myself before I go   love

let's travel and pretend we've seen a horror
so I can write it   love

I'm pushing at the outer reach of language
I can barely hold your hand

love   I see your window from a bed
that isn't mine or yours

I am not saying that this was in this city   I am not saying it was in this hotel   I am not saying it was people who I met here   I am just saying that sometimes you find yourself in your own bed   in the safety of your own body   and sometimes you realise that a notyou a somebodyelseyou   a newyou is exploring things the you in your own bed had never even thought of

JUST BECAUSE I DO THIS, DOESN'T MEAN

not knowing names doesn't make it something less
the midroad fight over red jumper and bike doesn't make it something more
it was just

    a long walk through see saw streets
    a stomach stretched tight as drumskin over hollow abdomen
    mouths finding every part of one another

    watching the mirror like a laptop screen
    a moon that kept trying to light us but kept off
    a room full of shortflightstopover

    the one who wanted to pretend he was wrestling
    to be pinned under the anxious face of the clock   watching
    the kisses that wanted to stay for longer than a night

    the one who said he wants to be a writer
    in the way an old woman in slippers
    might say she used to want to be a dancer

    the heavy scent of them as they showered and I dressed
    running until I was breathless in the centre of town
    it wasn't the rain   the rain hadn't come yet   but it would

Jamie Clayborough

Biography

Jamie Clayborough is an artist, occasional writer and foodie. He is obsessed with Bowie and is a trained sommelier. His guitar skills are less exemplary, but he's getting there. He can make a mean macaron.

An Evening with the Filmmaker

I can still taste black coffee if I flick the tip
of my tongue across my mouth and into my cheek.
I want the taste of you there instead.

I can still see the accent thick on your lips
in smokey downlit silences. Your smile
courtsies with sculpted contours.

I still hear the influence of film reel revolutions,
and celluloid war. It's a taste that sits
longer than I'll have to savour this.

Okechukwu Ndubisi

Biography

Okechukwu Ndubisi is a poet and writer. His work has appeared in *Agenda* and *The Literateur*, among other publications. An original memeber of Young Enigma and one of our 2013 LGBT History Month Writers-in-Residence, his radio play 'Me and Alan' was broadcast on Roundhouse Radio in 2013 as part of his LGBT History Month commission. He is currently working on his first novel.

TURINGERY

If

*

Immaculate in intent, he was
immaculate in intent. But clean things
like a canvas plead for intervention
in such circumstances

*

It's thinking. Great
ideas percolate in its arteries like
trouble in mind. It's a great idea. Listen:

If

*

The knack is a kind of sequestering:
cordon off the means from mealy-
mouthed emotions and watch:
invention tapers in,
a glistening pristine, if given clear
nights. Listen:

If he can speak to us

*

It's alchemy taking place. Inexact
and on the wrong side, errors
marginally clandestine, as with all things things chemical
impurely. He is riddled with love.

It's a kind of alchemy and someone
will be just the same. Or can you hear the clink
of coins about to change
their masters? Listen:

If he can speak to us across the abyss

*

How many ways can we formulate
grief? Sterling hope? See
how the codes shift over the years;
the words, evasive gears.
Run the algorithm again, for
I think that if he saw himself today
he'd smile
giving as a bed, fresh
from sharing, the rustle of sheets
a twinkle in the eye. Listen:
If he can speak to us across the abyss
what can die?

Listen: we can break. The same
caught diction now intimates
victorious rest.
Run the algorithm,
run the algorithm: see,
the photographs of him insist;
archives, diaries, love letters stammer to attest
that pure intent a triumph. He doesn't
struggle anymore, he just
gets on, gets on.

There are Moments

There are moments between us
when the distance between us
is only the thickness of two t-shirts.

And if I were to lay my head upon your chest,
the ins-and-outs of your breath
I would know like my own.

The Metal and the Mystery
or
On a Relationship That Didn't Work Out

The metal and the mystery, the balance and the bolts of this mess, this mass
    were wrought by countless evenings and by hands, desperate,
as with a chisel chasing beauty through the brass.

Life it gave, and took: consumed both masters in experimental flame—ours—
    and, for this fee and fuel, which we gave, dancing from our hands,
exhausted love which gazed at heaven, and chattered to the stars.

Down have I bent, and broken, worked, re-worked and torn apart
    to particles our making, searching, searching for the what's-not-working,
cracked the engine, leaked the oil, thick and holy, secret as heart's dark

blood. I thought that I would recognise the Wrong.
    But chisels cannot choose to save what I have chased away:
all hope of hope, the clatter of bird-flight, a long-sung song.

THE GLASSBLOWER

It's a *his* thing in hand:
his spindly fingers hold, blow, control
a mellifluous firebrand.
But see:
even though the heat is breathing,
solidity dreams of a seamless cold,
of having a childless hold on him. He knows—
his hot glow thinks, hints, winks . . .

Hardness will have its way with him
—it will harshen
him. It will wake one day,
and be breakable. Watch:
he will give away all those things which were soft.

But here, in his tender hearth, he's alive:
the fire's still wise, the fingers, quick in bliss;
won't stumble or hurt, won't blunder:
they're working, wombing, watching, that way and this—
eyes in wonder, singing, the *he* of him
in there still, softly hymning.

MIXING MOVEMENT

this is as good as it gets
for a man who could never dance
to dance
with the dream
with new york
peppa labeija
anji xtravaganza
willi ninja

to press his nose up against performance

step in time with them
dawn crandell
orbit them
patrick carroll-fogg
the way seahorses orbit one other when they're fascinated
you too, sequoia rose

and just look at them,
look at them go—they've got everything:
darren suarez
the things
javier ninja
their bodies don't know
darren pritchard
aren't worth noting.
peter grist
note the curve,
genevieve say
the torture and the nod for ecstatic release;
zinzi minott
the strive, the reel and the catch;
alyx steele
the stretch, the step
joshua hubbard
and the reach and what's achieved

KISS

And now, a kiss is not a kiss. Only this
remains me: just the word, now, tapering out into only air,
now, so, so sharp at the tip—so, it shows me lonelier, there.
Only this: it's

got a *kick* at the start, like a heart-
beat, only
it sighs, doesn't fight, now;
it fizzles.
And me in the middle, awaiting there
the promised kick, me
looking out for a kiss to meet

LETTER TO MY YOUNGER SELF

Sixteen, but you're direct. Obedient, but tides and sunsets
will have no more will. Quiet
and reserved, you osmote wisdom and mistakes, observe
the greats in books, see how they aggregate
towards the good. You know
you'll perish in stasis, and your brow tightens to atone:
so many things you thought you knew. You hope
that what you lack, perseverance synthesises. But ah, you
have a twinkle in your eye just yet. You've
a consciousness. You have deciphered that
love
is one thing, and not another.
Proceed.

And those eureka moments: rarified,
holy and implacable as infra-red invisible, those demands
you make with your eyes. You learn what can communicate
through lines of sight untrammelled,
the crowds immaterial, words immaterial, immaterial
his indifference—Okey,
you have in your crosshairs the stillness between thoughts,
the mind hurtling towards the next thing, the eyesight
catching a universe, deer-in-the-headlights, belied.

I WISHED

at first, for
a hero, of course.
I had a Hercules in mind,
the kind of man for whom
horses take wings,

and so might I. But a horse
is a horse is a horse and how awful
that you can lead him to water,
and make him think
it's the sky.

Oh, heaven.
Defend me from the might
of early wishes. I have been haunted
by the whispers of first kisses.
The moment I sink into the rhythm of things,
I hear the beating of wings.

FOAL

For 'Foal' by Tessa Pullan

Little foal, little wooden foal,
made with love:
I know as well as you the shapes
your master put you into. I, too
am a new-born thing,
legs askew,
and his face on mine.

He makes me hesitant and keened, yes
he does it to me too.
He makes my legs bow.
He makes me fall back
down at my own old feet.

He opens me up and turns me
inside out, examines me
like a dance for fault—

look! You can see the steps,

like yours,
small
and lonely.

14 April 2012

I

Nor night, nor day, no rest.
      Three times, three hours' sleep
Was all I could get. And on the day, only time for the suggestion,
      Only the hint of breasts: a 'loose Britney' and a deep
Neckline alone could attest
      To a female form.

II

It was neither falling nor flying. It was more
      Like the flourish—quick, pragmatic, really—of something with wings
By its sides, as hands in pockets; or the flick of a horse's
      Tail. It's all slick waves, unnecessary sheen, the mind on other things.
It's not impressive. It was more like the buck of something imprisoned
                under skin, poor
      Thing. Only too long tucked in.

III

So much of sex is born of fancy dress,
      And borne through by it into what comes after.
Skin wants only skin to hide beneath. And how it hides! Oh,
            we draw expressions
      On, and nothing is untrued. Even laughter
Tells: we are never ourselves. Unless
      that night discovered skin on skin: me, not yet a woman, loose,
           hastily done; him, the soulmate I
           met in an evening, and never saw since.

Markie Burnhope

Biography

Markie Burnhope is a poet, editor and activist whose work has appeared in print and online. They are the author of two chapbooks: *The Snowboy* (Salt Publishing, 2011) and *Lever Arch* (The Knives, Forks and Spoons Press, 2013). Their debut full collection, *Species*, was published in 2014 by Nine Arches Press.

THE UNIVERSAL 'WRONG BODY':
MY OWN NON-BINARY TRANS NARRATIVE

Note: This is a slightly-edited version of a piece I originally posted to my blog, Naming the Beasts. *It describes my own path, journey, and relationship with my own disability and gender. Other disabled people will have different responses to theirs. Some will feel the need to embrace their assigned gender with pride. Disabled women—especially disabled Black women and Women of Colour—may feel that identifying as a cis Woman is the most crucial response to an ableist, disempowering, disgendering society that they could possibly embody. Disabled cis men who have been demasculised by an ableist society may want to exert and emphasise their masculinity as their response. My conclusions on my own gender should not be taken as criticism or erasure of other disabled people's choices. But they might offer a path to others who have felt like me, and see no value in being stagnant.*

TW: gender dysphoria, disabled body issues, sexual dysfunction, systemic and interpersonal ableism, abuse, miscarriage

I am non-binary, genderderqueer, and trans.

I am non-binary, genderqueer, because my body, my embodiment experience, does not fit into, and has not been historically gendered as, 'man' or 'woman' *as the non-disabled world defines and describes it to me.*

I am trans because my experience, acceptance and conceptualisation of my body has had to transcend the 'man' / 'woman' binary. It has had to go beyond that binary for societal, political, personal and private reasons. The types of embodiment, categories and boxes handed down to me by non-disabled cisnormative culture and society are no longer useful, no longer anything I can take pride in. So I've abandoned them. I can't fit. I don't fit. And I've become far more confident, secure and at peace with myself since I realised I don't need to try anymore. I can carve out my own gendered embodiment space and occupy it, paint the walls, put posters up, leave and come back as and when I please.

There was always something different about me. Everyone who has ever talked to me knows this. But it took me all this time to figure this much out, especially because I didn't think my life had been like other trans people's lives I had read and heard about. Did I even have gender dysphoria, something I thought was required for me to even have the right to identify as trans?

The most common trans narrative is that if you suffer bodily dysphoria—that is, an intense, deep understanding that your innermost self does not align with the sex you were assigned at birth—you are not cis. You are trans. This narrative is summed up by the phrase 'born in the wrong body', and is particularly understandable in cases where people are deeply troubled that their bodies don't match their internal sense of self. They may experience mental health problems, self-harm, phantom pain. In everything that they are, they know that the gender they were assigned, based on their genitals and a wholly inadequate binary model of biological/physiological/scientific sex, is wrong (I won't cover it now, but plenty of evidence suggests that narrowing us down into two sexes excludes people who are intersex, and also people who have various disabilities and conditions which present them with bodies that veer from prescribed gender 'criteria').

This physical, bodily dysphoria is the one that most people wanting to know what being trans 'feels like' will read about.

I now know that one doesn't have to feel bodily dysphoria to identify as trans—a mere disassociation with your assigned sex is enough, on whatever grounds. But leaving that aside for a second, what do you do if you were born in what is universally considered 'the wrong body'? Because in terms of gender alone—without taking into account the intersection of disability and gender together—the 'wrong' body and the 'right' body are still both *a non-disabled body*. Gender dysphoria (we are told) is an uncommon, unusual experience relative to most people's experience. Disability is not. But there are no lines drawn on your body to distinguish bits that are gendered from bits that are disabled. So how would you know?

For 32 years of my life, I have had gender dysphoria, and not known it. Why? Because the world was constantly telling me, 'Of course you're in the wrong body; I would hate to live in your body. If I lived in your body, I would kill myself.' This sentiment is normalised, widespread, and reaches into the lives of disabled people on every level, from personal relationships and social participation to corporate and government policy. We are in the Universal Wrong Body. If we do suffer gender dysphoria at all, how can we possibly separate that bodily disparity from the message: *your body is inconvenient, freakish, and unwelcome?* Non-disabled public and politicians alike are even out in full daylight, debating whether we deserve our social security because our bodies simply aren't necessary to our society. They are superfluous. We are being triggered and made to believe we don't deserve to exist at every turn.

So there we are: I've had dysphoria. All my life. Bodily gender dysphoria? I don't know. Mental and social dysphoria? Slightly easier to disentangle. But to all intents and purposes, my gender is Disabled. For as long as I can remember I've felt no need to defend any identification as 'man' but every need to defend my identification as 'disabled person'. I am so proud of being a disabled person. It was there when I was born and will be there when I've gone.

'Non-binary' and 'genderqueer': words handed down to me by non-disabled society (as are so many things, until it's impossible to disentangle what we were coercively lead to believe, and what we chose) to describe a gender which falls in between or outside the male/female binary; a gender which is both, neither, or all. I also have other words to describe my gender which acknowledge that it's inseparable from disability. This has been my body from birth. I don't know where my disabled body ends and my gendered body begins. Nobody ever told me where to draw the line between them, and if they did, I'd consider it arbitrary. I have lived my gender through the filter of disability. I've seen the world through the lens of disability.

Two of these words are 'dis-cis' and 'disgender'. Both words share the prefix 'dis' found in the word 'disabled'. And that prefix has the same function. Neither word necessarily means 'not cis/ trans'. They might just mean 'made less cis' or 'made less gendered'. But crucially, they mean what society *has made me*, during a lifetime's exposure to oppression, whether my own in the form of ableism, or others' (Hydrocephalus gives me a certain amount of hypersensitivity to emotionally traumatic stimuli—I consider myself less an individual than part of a disabled community; when that community hurts, I hurt).

To explain these disabled-gender words, I need to go to the social model of disability. The social model is a reaction to the dominant medical model of disability, which everyone knows, and most people are perfectly familiar and comfortable with. It says that we have disabilities and conditions, and they are what's 'wrong with us'. We have afflictions, malfunctions, dysfunctions, to be cured. Our bodies are machines to be fixed.

In contrast, the social model relocates the source and cause of our 'disability' to society. We have impairments: our physical and mental disabilities, conditions and illnesses. They cause us pain, and none of us are exempt from the possibility of experiencing that pain. But our Disability, or disablement, comes from the inability of our bodies to participate fully in the world. Disability becomes not what's inherently and solely our fault and responsibility, but the ways in which we are oppressed: factors such as lack of access—to buildings, jobs, relationships, independent living, adequate medication, treatment and healthcare, housing, financial security. Prejudice, discrimination, stereotyping, patronisation, sentimentality, erasure. Ableist slurs, hate speech, hate crime, government law and policy. A history of freak shows, institutional sex abuse, eugenics.

These have been our disablement. Our bodies bear the brunt of it, but they are not its inevitable cause or reason. Our bodies can't be fobbed off as an inevitable reason for our disablement; otherwise we would be prejudiced against people due to all sources of pain, from a headache to a stubbed toe, and, by and large, we're not. We do not need to 'understand how hard it is' for non-disabled society to accept us. We do not need to relent and accept that society 'fears what it doesn't understand, and that's OK'. It's not OK. It all accumulates and amounts to our Disability. So under the social model, 'disabled' does not mean 'unable'. Disabled is what we are made. Another word to describe it could be 'disempowered'.

For me, this disempowerment has extended to gender. It includes demasculisation, or, if you like, 'dis-masculisation' (male privilege notwithstanding: if I am gendered as 'male' by others, I can benefit from that privilege in certain situations, even if I feel internally, negatively misgendered. This is all about my internal understanding of myself).

The line between 'cis' and 'trans' is blurred and complicated when your entire body is marked as culturally, economically, politically and physically undesirable, 'wrong', by a vast cultural standard, even a global standard. Over a lifetime, I've been slowly and gradually made 'dis-cis', 'disgender': constructively dismissed from the non-disabled, normative gender binary.

How, exactly? What are the details? To answer that would take an entire book, but here are a few:

One of my physical disabilities (apart from Hydrocephalus—I am also neurodiverse)—is Spina bifida, a spinal birth defect causing, among other things, some paralysis, with loss of sensation, on the lower half of my body. This has meant what is known as sexual 'dysfunction' by non-disabled standards. I find erections difficult to achieve. I very rarely ejaculate. Incontinence is a by-product. So I've discovered that sexual activity which does not involve my genitals is far less stressful, and much more pleasurable (I won't go into the kinks I prefer!). In fact, I'm at the point now where if I never involved my genitals in sex again, if I never even saw my genitals again, I would be perfectly content with my sex life.

This is queer and non-normative in a cisheteronormative society—especially in a 'male' world which is obsessed with penetrative sex, and equates your proficiency in that activity with your success as a man. Cis heterosexual men often have difficulty 'figuring out' how gay women who 'can't perform penetrative sex' (hint: they can), have any pleasure at all in sex. What do they even do, and what's so great about that? I laugh when I hear their question. But I don't feature in their worldview. When they ask, 'How do you have sex?' (and they do), I'm being addressed as a cripple, not as a queer.

In many ways, I've not qualified as a man socially. I don't have a job. I can't work, mostly due to Hydrocephalus (and a range of cognitive difficulties), depression and anxiety. I'll probably never work again. Therefore I will never be a 'breadwinner'. I am not the only person assigned male at birth who won't be a breadwinner, but as a disabled person I'm in a class of people who are far less likely to have access to sustainable supported employment across the world (especially women, and, most of all, disabled Black Women and Women of Colour).

Access to benefits and financial security for disabled people in the UK is being bulldozed. We are being fed the lie that entrepreneurship, ambition and aspiration towards a more empowered life is one which is achievable through personal responsibility, by chasing after stability and freedom. David Cameron's 'Paralympic Legacy' after London 2012, like his Big Society, was designed to project these ideas, and it failed. In fact, both the Big Society and Paralympic Legacy are national embarrassments now which nobody—if they haven't been sleeping under a rock—mentions anymore. The overwhelming pressure to contribute to the economy *as a moral responsibility and obligation* or be condemned as a lazy 'scrounger', part of the Something-for-Nothing Culture, has dogged me all of my adult life. And it's come to a head during David Cameron's government.

So being called 'man' just feels wrong. A woman in the street will say to her child: 'Move out the way while the man in the wheelchair gets past', and I'll recoil from the words. Because she is treating me with respect (or rather, refusing to patronise me) by seeing me as a 'man'. But I've had far too many experiences, throughout my life, where people (mostly men) didn't. In fact, I often felt they had me pegged as 'boy'. They would speak down to me, then up at their male friend standing at the same height, and the difference would be clear. Shopkeepers and barbers and barmen would call me 'buddy', 'pal', 'boss'—masculine words, but ones which grate because I also heard them referring to kids that way, and in exactly the same tone of voice. People would often treat me as a 'man' in a way they didn't treat men who were 'dark, tall and handsome'. Or even able-bodied, fair, short and unattractive (indeed, social cues made me feel as if I fell out of the 'attractive' / 'unattractive' binary completely).

If I go back into childhood, I remember being 'different'. I hated football as I thought it represented competition, one-upmanship, and (I was told even before I could understand them) racism, sexism and homophobia. I loved drawing and painting, reading poems, music. I loved activities that didn't require me to have to perform in front of, or measure up to, my able-bodied male friends (the possible exception was playing the drums, but even then, it's not something I felt I needed to compete at: only one or two of my friends played drums as well). I loved different kinds of toys, gendered male and female: Teenage Mutant Ninja Turtles and Bucky O'Hare, but also Glow Worms and Sylvanian Families. I once bought a rainbow cap from the Back to the Future ride at Universal Studios, whose colours moved around when you pressed the surface of the cap with your finger. I had a lime green and neon pink scooter. I had a shell suit in exactly the same colours. I shamelessly loved nature walks (what boy doesn't?) but would make daisy chains on the school field, hiding them behind my hand so that the boys couldn't see.

I loved *The X-Files*, and idolised Mulder and Scully not just because they were kickass but because they were helping to form my identity. In them I saw aspects of myself: the problematic, imaginative dreamer aware of a vast network of paranormal conspiracies, and the deeply spiritual sceptic with equal amounts of warmth and snark. It didn't occur to me they were 'male' and 'female'. They were just ... me.

None of these things necessarily equal transgender. By themselves, they probably equal 'odd boy'. And some of what I was as a child could be called 'disabled' rather than 'gendered'. But that is entirely my point. Disability and gender: they held hands. One was contained in, not separate from, the other. I didn't play with dolls. I didn't wear makeup. I didn't wear dresses (I don't think). But I was different. I was soft. I wanted to escape the clamour, oppression and stress of all that the non-disabled world told me I had to be to validate my humanity. I wanted to be nothing but myself.

There is one memory that will always stay with me, and it's just a snapshot. It may even be a combination of two memories. At preschool, we all had designated coat hooks, and each one had a picture on it to help us remember it each day. The picture on my coat hook was of a daffodil. I remember standing by it, my mother helping me on with my coat, and saying, 'When I grow up to be a girl ... ' I don't remember what I said after that, but I was clearly convinced for a while as a child that I would change gender when I grew up.

And now? Here I am. At 32, I'm still trying to grow: to unlearn, dismantle, pick apart and push against the stuff society imposed on me that didn't feel authentic, and take up stuff that does. Stuff which makes me happy, rather than asking other people whether happiness is what I should be feeling right now. After the last several years of seemingly lurching from one existential crisis to the next—every cry of 'Who am I, and where is God now?'—I suddenly feel as if I'm finally getting to answer the question.

Not long ago, but before I consciously thought of myself as having a feminine aspect, I started calling God 'She', and seeing Her as conceptually feminine. I started to address poems to 'my familiars': Quasimodo, Pinocchio, Queequeg. A range of animals. An angel. Champa the Moon Bear, a female Asiatic Black Bear, and the first bear ever to have keyhole brain surgery to implant a shunt for her hydrocephalus (a disability that we share). The lizards and mantises I have as pets. These projections of myself were not always female, or even human. But wherever my 'gender' was among them, it was clear that I had entered a new phase of exploring my identity in a way I had never felt the freedom to do before.

The most pivotal of these projections was Thomas-Mark or Evie-Lyn, the son or daughter my wife and I could have had. My wife (my partner at the time) had a miscarriage three years ago, at Christmas. All my adult life I had been told by doctors that because of my disabilities, my sexual dysfunctions, I shouldn't expect to have children. So I had given up on the idea, resolved that I would never be a father. But then it happened . . . almost. We had considered it a miracle. I still consider it a miracle, a fleeting one in itself but one that changed me from then on.

The first poem I wrote about Thomas-Mark or Evie-Lyn was 'The Snowboy'. It became the title poem of my first pamphlet. And then I wrote the others, and each one was a similar imagining and projection of, firstly, what my child might be like as male or female, and then what different-gendered Others, maquettes and monuments of myself, might be like. This piece isn't really about poetry. But that poem about a small snowman, about Thomas-Mark and Evie-Lyn, turned out to be very much about me.

I recently changed my Facebook profile picture to one that says: 'Don't assume I'm female. Don't assume I'm male. I am genderqueer. I am both, I am neither, I am all.' In my profile under 'religion', I've written St. Paul's words: 'I have become all things to all people.' At the moment it's meaningful in terms of the fact that my somewhat fluid sense of gender has opened me up to a new way of relating to the world and others (and more others than I've been able to for a long time, having lost trust in many 'friends' and 'allies' along the way).

On social media I've changed my name to an uncommon but established gender-neutral or feminine form: Markie (also used by TV actress Markie Post, if you wanted to look that up). I decided on this name in one night of Googling. I've asked some of the people I think will understand to call me Markie, hoping that everyone gets used to it and it just becomes . . . my name (it's not much of a stretch, to be fair: "ie" written down but, to the ear, still the nickname some people, like my dad, have called me all my life). My name will still be Mark on the books I've published so far. And well, that's OK.

People have asked me what pronouns I prefer. I've asked them not to use masculine pronouns ('he'), out of respect that I've made this change. I've told people I'm particularly drawn to the gender-neutral 'they' / 'their' / 'them', and the feminine 'she' is also fine, but I'm not going to enforce any of this; just call me by my name, please.

I'd be on top of the world if you did too.

Thank you for reading,

Markie Burnhope

LEO ADAMS

BIOGRAPHY

The youngest writer in our anthology, and one with a surprisingly distinct voice already, Leo is a sixteen-year old genderqueer poet from the West Midlands. He's loved writing all his life.

THINGS I HAVE LEARNT IN MY RELATIVELY SHORT AND MUNDANE LIFE

i.
when you cross the road,
do not gaze at the cars.
When you step into the oncoming traffic
do not stare the swerving drivers down and think,
well,
come on then.
Those headlights are not an invitation.

ii.
You are not an unfinished script;
there are no cameras here
and the false tears,
the single drop rolling down a cheek in a darkened cinema,
they are not for you.
They will never be for you.
The sobs choked back in your wake will be different -
there is no romance in hospital corridors.
You will not be picked up and fixed;
you are not broken.

iii.
It takes seven years for all your cells to die and renew.
One day you can look in the mirror and
know
he was never on you.
That all traces of his hands on your skin
and the whispers he left in your ear, carelessly, have fallen away.

iv.
there is a reason to open your eyes.

RUMINATIONS WRITTEN ON THE BACK OF AN EXERCISE BOOK

There's a boy.
He sits at the back of my English class,
chewing his pen and sneaking glances at me
with a crooked ink-blemished smile.
I wonder how many words the blue patch on his bottom lip
could have made,
and if any of them were my name;
the navy stain of possibility is as close
to my name being on his mouth
as it will ever be.

This is the only context in which it is not forbidden.

BLINDFOLDED

Oh, to touch you.
To map the constellations of freckles
On the sky of your skin with bare hands
And to name each star,
Claim it as my own,
Oh, to hear the quick-slow in-out of your breath
As my fingertips leave firework trails against you.
Against the soft swell of your thighs,
Stretch-marks—purple contours giving me indication that I don't need.
Because I know you blindfolded,
Know your body blindfolded.
Each scar is an aeroplane trail
Leading I know not where,
Yet through time they fade while kisses remain.
I live for these moments;
Stolen moments in late morning sun, tangled in sheets,
Or late at night with only streetlamp light
Seeping through thin curtains
To guide my trembling hands over you.
But darling, I could do this in pitch dark -I know you blindfolded.
I Remember Everything (a poem)
I remember everything about you.
Everything; from the way the sunlight dappled on your bare
Legs in the summer when we lay under the sycamore tree
Your father planted and how
Every breath of air
Seemed somehow sweeter because you were next to me.
I remember the sound of the ocean
As I laid my head on your sand-gritted shoulder
And if you told me then, I would have laughed at the notion
That I'd be back here in years to pass
Flinging my fears at the sea the way you flung your parting words to me.
I remember the taste of your mouth, and how it was different in the back yard
Of my parents' house than it was in the passenger seat

Of your dad's old blue Cadillac car.
And I remember you used to hate driving,
But that time I came home late with a bleeding head
Smelling of alcohol and someone else's low-tar cigarettes
You put aside your hurt to focus on my need and drove me
All the way to the emergency room, and stayed and reminded me to breathe
While they sewed up my head and I tried to sew up our relationship
But even though when we drove home
That morning just after six
And you told me this was something I couldn't fix
Every breath of air seemed somehow sweeter because you were next to me.

MAISY MORAN

BIOGRAPHY

Maisy Moran was born in 1993 in Birmingham. She studied English and Creative Writing at Birmingham City University, and identifies as a lesbian. Maisy spends the majority of her time either reading or writing, but she's also very keen on music—particularly Johnny Cash.

Keeps Turning

Like most people, I find myself wondering about abstract things. I wonder if one day instead of land we'll own acres of sky, and if we'll harvest the rain. I wonder if the eyes of my mum's Hummel dolls follow me as I walk by, and if they ever secretly listen in. Another thing I wonder is if musicians know where their songs are playing. By that I mean, do they know that their voice could be present at a wedding or at a funeral? That someone that they don't even know considers it 'their song', as though it were written exclusively for them? Do they know that their voice, their words, bring forth tears or encourage a smile as they evoke a memory in someone, be it of a certain person or of a specific day? In a sense, Tom Waits was a witness to the moment when everything changed between my dad and me.

Dad was dying. He'd been dying for a long time. It was almost like he had changed his name, and we were all gradually getting accustomed to it. He was a whole new person. After almost a year of dying, it was hard to imagine him living. I don't think he was in that final year. Technically speaking, yes he was, but that's all. It's a big waiting game, and I was more than prepared. Every time the telephone rang, the first thing that would cross my mind was that it had happened and that I should check my suit still fitted.

I visited as often as I could over that year. Hannah came with me at the start, trying to be supportive. Then she came less and less. She found it too hard. It wasn't her dad dying, it was mine, but for Hannah it was too difficult. I never called her out on it, yet we both knew she didn't have a headache and that her sister hadn't spontaneously rang and was coming over with the boys. Hannah just didn't like my dad as the dying man. Few of us did.

These visits were once a week. Every Tuesday. After I finished work at half past five, I stopped off there on my way home. I would let myself in, make a cup of coffee in the kitchen, and then announce myself by letting myself into their bedroom. Mum was always at the foot of their bed, reading a book whose front cover was as wrinkled as she was, as though the books she pulled from her shelf had all aged along with her. Dad would be in bed, the long hairs of his chest creeping up like ivy out from beneath his striped pyjama shirt, his hands folded over his stomach. He would raise three fingers in response to my greeting. Not once did he smile at me; he never gave the impression that he was pleased to see me. Mum did. She acted as though I hadn't visited in ages, as if I didn't come over every single week. She would set her book to one side, get up and hold me. I hated that because, again, it made me wonder. Was I now the only one who would hold her back?

It was Tuesday 5th October 1999. The windows were freckled with raindrops. It was quarter past six. Hannah would call me at half past to check where I was so then she could heat something up for me to eat when I got back. Usually at this time, I would help mum wash up dad's dinner plate, scraping most of the sodden mushy remains into the bin. Dad, a man who was known for asking if you were finished with your food before helping himself, rarely finished a meal in those days. Mum was standing at the sink, looking out of the window at her garden, or rather what remained of it. When dad's health declined, so did her flowers. Two of her loves withered away simultaneously. I really felt for her.

'Adam, I need some milk,' she said.

She may as well have spoken in another language. It felt bizarre for someone with a dying husband to be talking about something as mundane and domestic as shopping. I hadn't heard her speak about something so normal and so present in such a long time, it sort of took me aback. When dad got sick, mum latched onto the past; she used her every breath to reanimate it for us, talking with such warmth about the brighter days, those that had not been tainted by the grime that came with the reality of terminal illness. So it took me a minute or two until I could respond.

'Sure,' I said.

'Take him with you.'

Again, I faltered. I knew who she was talking about but I wanted to know why. Why did I have to bring my father with me to buy some milk? He had never done it for her even when he was in good health. I remember the one and only time she had sent him up to the shop to get her something (it could have even been milk),

149

and he had come back with a magazine instead. It wasn't that he was forgetful or that he had done it out of spite. It was simply because he was just like a big child who took advantage of having money in his pocket. Mum didn't bother asking again. From then on I was the one she would send.

The only reason I could think of for her asking this of me, was that she wanted me to take him out on a drive, give him one last swig of the world outside. Dad didn't move around much but he could if he really wanted to. Soon that wouldn't be the case. He'd be unable to do anything, not even drag his feet down the hall to the toilet, and maybe he wouldn't be home at all in a few weeks or months time.

'Okay,' I said.

Twenty minutes or so later, Mum was standing on the doorstep, seeing us off with the dishcloth cool and limp like a dead fish in her hands, as I buckled myself and dad in. She didn't wave, she only smiled. I think she was scared that if she moved she would break, that the cloth was a sort of sellotape that was just about keeping her in one piece.

Dad did nothing. He just stared straight ahead, his face vacant and his eyes pale like a shirt that had been washed too many times. They didn't seem to look at or focus on anything. Well, they certainly didn't look at mum or me.

As we reversed off the drive, I raised my hand in a motionless wave. The car was filled with the sound of gravel crunching beneath the wheels, and then it was only the vehicle itself making noise as we drove away. Rather than go to the shop around the corner, I went to the one that was at least twenty minutes away. Dad didn't seem to notice. I had expected him to protest in some way, not only about which shop we went to but about going out at all in the first place. Instead, mum had told him to go, and he had complied without a word, reaching out for us so we could heave him up and dress him.

I asked him if he wanted to have some music on. Usually, a question like that was met with an awkward slight turn of his head. It was a head balanced in the puddle of pink sore flesh that was his neck. His toothless mouth would part to let out a small huff, which he would clamp tightly shut with a short grunt, which meant no. But for whatever reason, that day his mouth remained open and he gave the feeblest excuse for a nod I had ever seen. I was briefly taken aback, and I think I felt relieved that I wouldn't have to spend the journey listening to the harshness of his breaths, a distorted version of the same breaths I had listened to as a boy when I would put my head on his chest as he napped on Sunday evenings after dinner, the smell of gravy on his breath, the grease of roast potatoes still slick on his fingers.

My dad was one of those people—he didn't like music. I never really took this claim seriously. To me, it was just another way for my dad to plump up this peculiar air around him, just another anomaly to make him seem more interesting and to probe curiosity. I'd never found any evidence to prove my conviction—not once had I caught him sneakily listening to one of mum's records, nor had I ever found a mixtape of mine from when I was a teenager hidden in his sock drawer. All the same I couldn't and still cannot fathom someone who is content to live a life without a tune.

I put on the CD that was still left in the car stereo. The music trembled off into a silence that was then resuscitated by the beautiful thrum of a piano in the next song. I wasn't expecting to get through the entire thing. I waited for dad to grumble and moan until I gave in and turned it off—he didn't. He was still, he was quiet, and he even looked . . . appreciative, as though he was actually enjoying it. When it ended, the final notes fading out, dad reached over to me and touched my arm.

'Put that one back on,' he said.

'What?' I glimpsed at him. 'You want to listen to that song again?'

Without a beat, he nodded.

There are many things you do for people who are dying. You pretty much say yes to every request they make. They want to engage with you in a deep conversation about the afterlife that is sure to haunt you all the way back home? You do it. They want you to watch that film with you that you can't stand? You do it. They want you to wipe their arse? You do it. Wiping his arse and playing that song again were in entirely different leagues, but you get my meaning. I didn't ask questions. I did it.

I brought it back and played that song again. Dad slowly

retracted his hand and exhaled.

> Well the band has stopped playing but we keep dancing
> The world keeps turning, the world keeps turning
> On his hand he wore the ring of another
> And the world keeps turning, the world keeps turning

And the song kept playing and the song kept playing. I think it had ran through three times before we had found a parking space in front of the shop. Dad didn't have to ask a second time. I'd see his head turn in the corner of my eye, his mouth agape with the question on his tongue, and I would beat him to it. Every time it started, dad sighed.

Tom's gritty voice choked out midsentence as I killed the engine. The air around us seemed to prickle like water after it hits a hot oven ring. I remember feeling awkward, not sure whether to make a remark or to just leave it. In the end, I went with the latter.

'Do you want to come in?' I turned to my father as I undid my seatbelt. I froze.

There were tears in his eyes, those same eyes that had seemed dry for so long, that had displayed no interest in the world or any of us for years, perhaps even before he got sick. He hadn't cried even when he had found out he was dying—that it had spread everywhere, there was nothing more they could do—at least not that I saw. The only thing that seemed to bother him was that he would miss out on seeing in the new millennium, which we hoped would not be the case since the end of the year was so close and his colour wasn't too off yet. Then for some reason, my dad was crying. He was crying in front of me in my car and what was more, it appeared that he was crying over a song.

I was speechless. I had said goodbye to my father a long time ago. I had believed that man that had raised me had faded away, and yet there he was, momentarily flushed again with colour, with life. I was immediately aware that this may be the last time I would ever see it, see him, and I didn't want to disturb it. There are some instances you want to physically grab, cut it out like a photograph in a magazine because they struck you, they stopped you from turning the page and you want to keep it. It's frightening how things disappear, how temporary everything is. Once it's gone, it's gone for good.

I contemplated speaking to him, reaching out and touching him, letting him know I was there and that it was okay . . . I wanted to but I couldn't. I was only able to stare.

His tears seemed ceaseless, as though his eyes were sweating out everything inside of him like a raging fever. He didn't cover his face, and I was touched that he hadn't felt the impulse to hide from me, to conceal this rare instance of weakness from his only son. His hands instead remained clasped over his belly, the tears rolling down to his chin, where they shivered for a few seconds and then dripped onto his shirt.

Other people came and left the parking lot. For us, no time passed and although we hadn't said a word to each other, I hadn't ever felt so close to him before.

Eventually, he took a deep breath. 'Adam?'

I straightened. 'Yes, dad?'

'Go and get your mother her milk.' That was all he said.

Afterwards we drove home without saying anything to one another, and we didn't listen to any more music. Dad adopted his pyjamas, the skin of the dying man, and went back to bed, where he would practically see out the rest of his days. I told no one of what had happened—not mum, not Hannah—and not once did I mention it to dad in the visits that followed, and he returned the favour.

The year came to an end, and dad slept right through the New Year celebrations. Still, he awoke in the new millennium and that was all any of us could ask for.

The telephone rang as I was getting ready for work on Wednesday 8th March. As soon as it started ringing, I took off my tie. I knew. I became a man without a father.

I hadn't thought about that drive for the longest time. Even when he died it hadn't crossed my mind. Not once. I suppose there was more to think about. I thought a lot about my mother. I worried for her constantly, and all I could think about was that I would lose her too. I dedicated a lot of my time after that Wednesday to arranging the funeral and helping mum move in with Hannah and me. It was only temporary; it was just until she took to life again.

A few years went by. I was cleaning out the car one Sunday afternoon while Hannah cooked dinner and I opened the glove compartment, rifling through all the CDs that had been stuffed in there. Some of them I didn't even know we owned, others I thought had been lost. Then there it was.

I sat in the driver's seat, put in the second disc, and found that song. Every time the song ended, I felt I could see him turning to look at me in the corner of my eye, and so I would bring it back. No matter how many times I played it, I couldn't be certain what had brought my dad to tears that day. I only hope that he was happy, and that he was okay with the world continuing to turn even after he was gone.

LUCY MIDDLEMASS

BIOGRAPHY

Lucy Middlemass is a young writer from Nottingham. Lucy is a tidy and wise person living a 1970s lifestyle in a 1980s house. She spends her time writing and editing. Her first novel, *Jinger Barley and the Murkle Moon*, will be published this year.

TRAMWORKS

The light cuts a line down my body. I nudge the fridge door with my hip and watch myself disappear. On the lit side, my stomach rolls over my pyjama bottoms and my wrist is as thick as the top of my arm. It's no better to be half a monster. I'd rather stay in the dark.

I open the fridge properly and don't look down at myself again. The shelves are full of food I used to eat. Although he shouldn't, my dad still brings it. Growing girls need to eat, he says.

There's a packet of sausages so swollen it's like they're bursting with liquid, and spreading my fingers out doesn't hide the similarity. Two cellophane-covered discs of ham and the rest of the cooked chicken sit on the shelf behind. Dad's new wife's children couldn't finish it on Sunday. I breathe the dull, savoury smell of the chicken through the foil. The cold has taken away its richness like it's been rinsed or submerged.

There's nothing wrong with holding it.

'You're not going to eat that, are you?' Chelsea says.

I thought she and Mum were in bed. My sister stands in the kitchen doorway with her arms folded and her coat on. The hall light spills into the room. There are muddy splashes up her jeans and her shoulders are shiny with rain. She's tucked her hair into a baseball cap and I wonder which of us our mum would shout at first if she came downstairs now.

'Why are you cooking in the dark?' Chelsea flicks on the main light, hurting my eyes. 'And what's that smell?' She will be able to see the whole of me now. 'You won't eat that, will you?' she asks again.

There are more sausages on the worktop, the packet sliced down the centre. Oil spits from the frying pan and slides down the dirty tiles so slowly it's hard to tell which drips are new.

It doesn't matter. Every surface is caked in grease and dust. There are torn cereal boxes, mugs with lip marks on the rim shaped like orange segments, a heap of teabags turning pale at the edges. Cat litter clings to my bare feet and black flies struggle to free themselves from the draining board.

'You hungry?' I ask. Chelsea's bound to be if she's been out.

'It's all for you if you want it.'

The chicken is heavy and cold in my hands and I don't want it near me, but the possibility of eating something is thrilling. I remember the beef burgers in the oven. There's relish in the fridge, that's what I was looking for.

'Not that hungry.' She comes over and pulls a strip off the chicken. It moves in my hands as she tugs. When she swallows, the meat will become part of her. It will be her. That won't happen to me again. She sucks her fingers and I wonder what stops her biting down.

'There's ice cream too,' I say. 'Not the crap stuff.'

'You like the crap stuff. I'm only back for a hammer. Amy is outside.'

It's after midnight. I'm more curious than responsible, and I'm not very curious. I'd better ask anyway. 'What do you need a hammer for?'

She doesn't need to tell me why Amy won't come in. The reason is all over the worktop, up the stairs, on the sofas, caught in the nettles outside. This isn't a house for visitors.

I turn off the oven and put the frying pan in the sink on top of our cutlery, saucepans and glasses. There's a hiss when I turn on the tap, and the half-cooked sausages float up in the bowl like they've drowned.

'There's a new car park where the tram will stop when it's finished,' she says. 'People are already using it.'

'You want to ... break into cars with the hammer?'

She says something about me being stupid as she opens the middle drawer. 'It's the money we want,' she says.

My sister's legs are so thin in those jeans. She hardly has a bottom. The money isn't in the cars.

There's no space between my thighs because I'm standing up. If I were sitting at the table, my fat would pool around me. At school, I don't want to stand or sit. It's £4.50 an hour—the council is coining it.

My school jumper is a ladies' size eighteen. A smaller one would cling to every bulge. It's like the council are the ones stealing.

'So we need to smash it open,' Chelsea says. 'Or maybe wrench

157

the back off with the other side of the hammer.'

'What?' I haven't been listening.

'The Pay and Display thing. It'll be full of coins, won't it?' She says it like it's free money and she and Amy are the only ones to have noticed. She leaves the middle drawer open and the hammer in her hand makes a shadow like a cartoon anvil on the kitchen floor. It suits her. Her plan is innocent and far-fetched. As if there won't be a camera.

'What do you think prison food is like?' I ask.

Chelsea has a reputation not a record, but that'll change. She'll be sixteen soon. The clothes at the back of her wardrobe have their security tags on, and she carries packets of feathery green drugs in her school bag. Her bedroom window is usually open, but it doesn't stop the sweet, smoky smell floating down the corridor. Maybe I am curious about what she does; it's not like she'd show me if I didn't go looking for it.

'You're not funny,' she says, although I wasn't trying to be. I was only wondering. 'We won't get caught.' She takes off the baseball cap and lays it on a sliding pile of newspapers that covers the table. It will stay there, which is silly because she could've used it to hide her face from the camera.

'Can I come with you?'

She shakes her head and counts the reasons on greasy fingers. 'No. You're thirteen and you'll slow us down. It's too late and it's too dangerous. Amy's my friend not yours. I'm supposed to look out for you.' And you're fat and ugly and everyone hates you.

She doesn't say the last part but I hear it. She's right about the rest too. I don't have any friends and my body isn't for running.

'And Dad's coming over to take you to that weight clinic in the morning,' she adds. That one doesn't get a finger so I know she means it.

'Please.' If I go to bed, morning will come sooner. The night will stretch if I fill it. The clinic doesn't work anyway, I've been a thousand times before. Four, at least.

'No way, Scarlett.'

'I'll tell.' I hate myself for sounding like a child. I think of levering open the back of the Pay and Display machine and hundreds of gold coins glittering around our trainers on the tarmac. It's not like they'd really let me be the one to do it, but I want to see.

'Okay then,' Chelsea says, more easily than I expected. She should know I'm bluffing. Who would I tell?

Dad's old coat is the only thing I can wear, so she hands it to me in the hallway. She hasn't noticed or doesn't care that I'm wearing pyjamas underneath. The lining of my trainers is worn away and rubs my bare ankles. When Chelsea opens the door, fresh air fills me.

'You've lost weight,' Amy tells me as we close the front gate. She stands in a circle of rain under the streetlight by our mum's car. She's only being nice. 'Did you get it?' she asks Chelsea. She doesn't ask what I'm doing here because I don't make any difference. She's tiny.

Chelsea pats herself on the lower back where she's tucked the hammer into the waistband of her jeans like a gangster. 'Yes,' she whispers. We could speak as loudly as we wanted in the kitchen. No one would have come downstairs.

We walk to the end of our street and cross the road. Looking both ways would only waste time. Although it's late and dark, it wouldn't be right for my sister to walk next to me because I'm thirteen and I'm fat and ugly. We all know that. In front, Chelsea holds herself awkwardly, and adjusts her jeans. Amy turns and walks backwards, hurrying us up, reminding us this was her idea. Mud is splattered up her legs too.

None of our neighbours' lights are on, and a dog barks behind someone's front door. Chelsea and Amy grab each other for a moment, but look back and let go, giggling. They'd be rubbish gangsters. The puddles shine black and we tiptoe over them.

Our route is caged by temporary walls put up for the tramworks, sometimes forcing us to walk along the road, sometimes on the pavement. I can almost feel them scraping against me. If they were any closer my flesh would squeeze through the mesh like ground mince.

'It'll be done soon,' Amy says. 'The paper said September. It's this way. We need to follow the tracks.'

Symbols and codes are daubed in neon writing everywhere we step. The paint looks fresh enough for us to make tacky footprints, but it's not. Someone must know what it all means. Gas here. Wires over there. Don't cut through that or drill near this. When the tram is finished we won't be able to walk along here but the pipes and cables will still be underneath. One of the pipes would be wide enough to crawl through if we could get down there. Next to the trenches, there's a mound of gravel and a pile of pallets, and huge concrete cylinders sit near a yellow digger.

'Come on,' Chelsea says to me. 'We haven't got all . . . day.' Amy laughs then Chelsea does too. Chelsea's sounds relieved, like she wasn't sure if what she said was a joke or a mistake. Amy's laughter told her it was okay. 'We haven't got all night,' she corrects herself, anyway.

Although it's dark, low clouds fill the sky ahead. I pull up Dad's hood, enjoying hiding somewhere my body can fit. Rainwater splashes onto my forehead and fills my eyelashes.

We cross another road. If it were light, I could tell Chelsea which house a boy from my class lives in. He wasn't the one who wrote fat bitch on my bag, but he laughed with the others. They didn't realise I could see why it was funny too.

At the end of another street, our route is blocked. Heavy machinery operates on this site, it says, and there they are, the tops of more diggers and other machines poking up behind corrugated walls, abandoned until tomorrow morning. Twenty-four hour security is in operation. We are strictly forbidden. Chelsea and Amy aren't bothered. They've only just come this way. They know where to go next.

A gap between two houses leads to a narrow footpath with branches either side that Chelsea lets fall back on me, then there's a concrete footbridge and a single van passes beneath us. It would be quicker to cross the playing field where we would see the swings and climbing frame turned grey in the dark, but instead we pick up the route of the tram again. Chelsea and Amy can't be distracted. The machine won't wait.

New metal tracks run through the car park of an old people's home and stop at its front door. This is the most finished stretch we've seen. The curtains have been taken down from most of the rooms upstairs and the spaces outside for cars are empty. No one lives here anymore.

'Hold on. I want to look. It'll be pulled down soon,' I say, risking them telling me they shouldn't have let me come. Chelsea warned me I'd slow them down, didn't she?

'We need to go behind the building and follow the tracks,' she says, the doubt in her voice telling me not to keep Amy waiting. Amy doesn't say anything because she hears it too.

'What if someone sees us?' Chelsea adds, knowing what her little sister worries about most. Doesn't she feel powerful enough with the hammer down her jeans? She's right, we mustn't be seen. We're more or less what the papers would expect us to be, even though we're girls.

There are more mesh barriers but a gap shows the whole building. Amy and Chelsea stand next to me with their hoods up too, shifting their feet because there is no Pay and Display machine here. There's no money to be made from visits to the elderly. Maybe not enough people do it. Maybe hardly anyone noticed the building was here until a group of parents complained about the tram going through the playing field, and it had to be diverted.

There's a notice on one of the downstairs windows, partly hidden in the shadow of an empty hanging basket. A picture of a tram with a crossed-out circle over it is printed halfway down, but we're too far away to read. There's a single bench in what's left of the gardens, too close to the new tracks to stay.

'There's nothing here,' Amy says. 'Come on.'

They walk away, their minds full of coins twisting and chiming into their cupped hands. I turn to follow them, ready to have my hands and mind filled too, but there's a woman coming from behind the old people's home. She sits on the bench, lights a cigarette, and stretches out her legs. Even I can see she's bigger than me.

'Scarlett. Come on,' my sister says or something like that, I can't be sure. They're heading around the other side of the building. They'd get caught if they shouted. It must be past one o'clock in the morning.

'Coming.' I'm not, but they won't hear me. They'll be round that corner, thinking I'm right behind them. They won't care enough to come back. There's a machine giving away free money if you have

161

a hammer.

My body makes a huge shadow across the car park of the old people's home. The council will take away the streetlights soon, and there will only be trams. They won't run this late, so no more shadows will fall. Maybe mine will be the last. The woman isn't watching me, she's flicking ash into the mud by her shoes.

I walk past the dead hanging basket and the notice on the window. The print is tiny, it's hopeless. It's like they never even tried. It's probably an office through there, tired furniture against the walls, a disconnected computer monitor on the floor. No more shuffling footsteps upstairs, no one flushing the toilets, no smell of meat and vegetables cooking on Sundays. Wherever the old people are now, they're not here.

The woman on the bench announces, 'I haven't got any money and I left my phone inside.' She's said it before, I can tell because there's no proper feeling in her voice. She's not afraid of me because she doesn't have anything I can take.

'It's okay.' She looks up, surprised to hear a girl's voice, maybe. 'I'm not here for anything like that.' It isn't quite true. I was on my way to do something exactly like that, but I'm not now. Chelsea and Amy have disappeared, the lure of coins stronger than ever. My legs are shaking because the rain has soaked through my pyjamas, but I was shivering in the kitchen too. You're bound to feel the cold, the woman at the clinic told me. And the man, the time before.

'Haven't you got a home to go to?' the woman on the bench says. It's more a telling-off than a question. 'It's late.' She sneezes without putting her hand to her face and sparks jump from her cigarette. Her plimsolls are dirty from walking on the mud now the home's grass is gone, and her feet hang over the tram tracks. If she did that in a month, she'd be cut off at the ankles and I'd be able to see circles of meat with white bone inside, like something hanging in a shop front.

I sit next to her. She's enormous and there is barely room on the bench. Parts of my body sink uncomfortably through the slats. She tilts herself as though she's moving over for me, but settles back down where she was.

'It's raining,' I tell her because it's the middle of the night and we're alone together.

She nods. 'It's late. How old are you?'

'Eighteen.' I might as well be so I say it. And, 'How old are you?' because if I really were eighteen, it'd be okay to ask. We'd both be grown-ups, wouldn't we?

'You look younger with your hood up,' she tells me, not answering my question. 'Have you run away? Where's your stuff?' She's looking at my huge legs, sounding only vaguely interested, like there's no way she could intervene no matter what was happening to me tonight. Maybe she works here and she's the one who chose the tiny font for the anti-tram sign.

'I'm out with my sister and her friend,' I say, before I realise I'm halfway to explaining our crime to a potential witness. *She told me she was eighteen,* I imagine her saying in court. *But I could tell. They're all liars.* It doesn't matter, it's not my crime anymore.

'Boys?' she asks, giving me an explanation I wish I'd thought of.

'Yes,' I say and try to picture the sort of boys girls like us might be meeting in the middle of the night. It's hard to get their faces right. They turn into the boys from school, the ones who write things on my bag and don't even pretend they didn't.

The woman on the bench must mistake my expression for worry because she says, 'I used to go to bed with my clothes on, shoes and all. I'd wait for Dad to start snoring. Then I'd take his keys out his jacket pocket, always on his chair in the lounge. Had to hold my hand so steady when I lifted them, terrified they'd make a noise and the game would be up.'

'Then what?'

'Then I'd be out, over the back fence and away.' The woman on the bench would barely get up a curb now. Whatever else she sees in my face makes her say, 'I wasn't always like this, you know.' It doesn't sound like regret, or if it is, it's no different from the way our mum used to talk about meeting our dad. Shiny-eyed like the future she'd imagined could still be found under the damp piles of newspapers or be let in, if only someone moved the boxes of empties blocking the back door.

'No, of course not,' I say. She'd probably like me to ask about the boys she snuck out to meet, maybe revealing she's married to one of them now. *All these years later,* she'd say.

'It's my sister and her friend. They're the ones with boyfriends,' I tell her instead.

Chelsea does have a boyfriend. He used to go on our bus but the route changed when they started digging. His dad works nights and couldn't take him and his sister, so they go to a different school now. In a few months Chelsea, Amy and I will be on the tram and it will be twelve minutes shorter than ever but they will still be at a different school.

'Oh. Well. I only came out for a fag,' the woman says.

'Do you live here?'

'I'm forty-four, sweetheart, not eighty. I'm from the flats over there. But I've been coming here for years.'

I don't tell her I thought maybe she worked at the home and had to sleep there to look after the old people. I'm not going to ask why she comes here in the middle of the night to smoke either. Maybe her husband disapproves and it's a secret, which is funny if he's the one she used to sneak out to meet. Or maybe she used to sit here with some old boy and puffed away while he prattled on about the roses or the war, and habits are hard to break, no matter what they are.

After a minute of silence she asks me if I'm hungry. 'You look it. I've got a Mars bar somewhere.' She swaps her cigarette into her other hand and pats her coat pockets. Her skin is red and dry, and rain runs through her fingers.

'No.' I haven't eaten anything like that in two years.

'Thought you might say that,' she says, like she knows me. Maybe people like us all know each other, and this is the first time I'm finding out.

'Have you tried to stop?' I ask. This must be why I'm not grabbing up the last pound coins and fifty pences right now with Chelsea and Amy. I wanted to ask this. I flatten my palm on my right knee so she won't see it shaking.

'The smoking or the eating? Actually, doesn't matter. Tried both. Wanted to for the kids. I've got two. One's built like his dad, and the other, five years old, is as thin as a whippet. Anyway, it didn't stick.' To prove her point, she starts eating the Mars bar. 'You?'

I like that she'd ask me, like I'm a person too, with things that might have happened to her. It's not the same at school. 'My dad is taking me to a clinic tomorrow. No big deal, I've been before.'

A police siren sounds in the distance, and I think of my sister. There must have been a camera. Mum will shout the house down, or she would if she could be bothered to answer the door to them. She gets up to go down the shops, and only then when she's run out of vodka. She wouldn't need to do that if either of us really looked eighteen. Maybe Chelsea will tell them Dad's address instead.

'Didn't think you were as old as you said,' the woman says, talking with her mouth full and smiling at me for the first time. There's chocolate smeared at the edges of her teeth. 'Or you'd take yourself. Well.' She stands up, and it's slow but looks easy. The wrapper falls off her coat because it no longer exists for her. 'This is me,' she says, as though it's her bus stop and she can't stay to talk. 'Good luck with it this time.'

Her body fills the space between the tramlines, and she walks along the tracks until she's at the home's door. She holds onto the wall and pants. She turns to step onto the mud and I see the flesh around her neck ripple as she gulps.

The wrapper drifts away from me, over the car park, and is caught in the wobbling mesh wall where two skinny girls are leaning with their hands full and their pockets sagging. They've pushed their hoods off, no longer bothered about the rain. I don't want them to see the woman. I want her to be fast enough.

'Hey, Scarlett, we got loads. Come on,' Chelsea says. The police car can't have been for them. They don't come any closer, as if walking across an abandoned car park would be worse than stealing the money.

'You go,' I say. 'I'm going to sit here for a bit.'

They laugh like Mum used to when she was drunk. Now she just drinks, she doesn't laugh at all. They probably stopped to smoke and there will be no point talking to them until tomorrow.

The woman is still walking towards the flats behind, her plimsolls sliding sideways over the mud. Chelsea and Amy are laughing too hard to notice her. My eyes are gritty and hot, and I follow them home because I've stretched the night as far as I can. I can hardly focus on their shapes in the dark.

Dad forgot my appointment at the clinic, and I was late. I mostly circled smiley faces on the form the receptionist gave me in case it made it go faster. He didn't look at it but it's safe in the filing cabinet with my other four. The girls I shared a room with told me I was fatter than them, which is how it works in places like that. A week later, Dad forgot to collect me.

*

Unpacking didn't take long. I'm wearing clothes in bed when Chelsea gets home, although there is no one to see. It's before midnight but they'll have spent the coins in a couple of days. She'll say going out is boring with no money. She slams a cupboard door in the kitchen, swears when she treads on something on the stairs and turns on her music in her room. The smell seeps under my bedroom door so strongly it's as though I can see it. I get up.

I don't need to lift the keys quietly out of anyone's pocket, or climb over the back fence. It's not raining tonight but I put Dad's coat on anyway. He didn't come back for most of his stuff, like he wanted to close the door on everything here. No one could blame him. His wife probably tells him to bring the food. She's seen what I look like, and must think I'd want it.

The streets are empty and the dog is quiet. The mesh walls force me onto the road, onto the pavement and onto the road again. Pipes and wires twist through the trenches beside me. I push the branches out of my way on the path. Two cars pass under the footbridge, and I lean on the railings until I see a third. There are no clouds, and the sky is full of stars. I look down and see splashes up my jeans. Chelsea and Amy followed the tracks and found what they wanted. I will too. The woman goes out to smoke every night.

I walk along the tramlines through the streets on the other side of the bridge. They turn a corner, and I turn with them. And they carry on, into the darkness ahead. There's nothing to stop them. The old people's home and the bench are gone. There's a piece of paper caught in the mud and if it's the anti-tram sign I don't want to see it. A lorry parked on the road is loaded with broken bricks and window frames.

Dad's hood hides my face as I walk home. I don't need to follow the tracks anymore, so I cut through the playing field. If there's bread in the freezer, I'll make cheese on toast when I get back. From the kitchen table, I'll be able to watch it bubble under the grill. It'll be crisp and salty, and it will stick to the roof of my mouth if I bite into it. I won't do that. I'll throw it away. I can see it on the overflowing bin already.

There's a figure on one of the swings and it's obvious I've found her. The chains are stretched around her body, and a red dot shows me the tip of her cigarette. My swing doesn't move when I sit down.

'Hiya,' she says. 'You come for that Mars? Luck would have it, I do have another.'

'No. I don't eat them.'

She shrugs. 'Did you hear what happened last week? Some kids broke into the Pay and Display at the new car park. Your sister wouldn't know anything about that, would she?' Her voice is steady.

'I told her not to do it. It's Amy, her friend, she's the one who makes her.' It's not true, not really, but Chelsea's my sister and our mum won't do anything.

'Well, I don't know anything about it. None of mine, is it?'

'Thanks.'

She moves her shoulders again because it makes no difference to her. 'What are you doing out here, then? If it's not crime, and it's not boys. And you don't want my chocolate.'

'I wanted to ask. I wanted to ask if . . .' If I'll become like you.

'We're not the same, if that's what you're worried about. I'm just greedy. You know what your trouble is, don't you?'

Everyone knows what my trouble is. They tell me at the clinic. It's why Dad brings the food. It's why the boys laugh when they write on my bag.

'But it'll kill you,' I tell her. 'What about your kids?'

What about Chelsea and me? The drink is killing Mum too.

'I'm not going to fight no more. You're not the same, you're still young. Don't give in to it.'

'I'm disgusting,' I say. My legs make a shaky shadow on the scraped grass under the swing.

A noise comes from the back of her throat, one which might mean she disagrees, or it might just be the fags. 'You can't weigh more than my five year old. Your trouble is you don't see yourself right.'

BLYTHE COOPER

BIOGRAPHY

Born in Bedford and living in Liverpool, Blythe Cooper is a charity worker by day and a creative by night. She works with words and image to create strong and moving pieces. Spoken word is a new obsession of hers, and she uses it as both an art and a catharsis. Blythe is currently collaborating with other artists to bring spoken word and slam poetry to new audiences for therapeutic impact.

To The Woman Who Will Never Meet My Mother

My mother loves you

My mother loved you before she even knew you were a woman
She knew you would be true to me
Would love me like she did, and then some

My mother planned for your arrival
Had chocolate and tissues ready for the days
        that we couldn't sing together
Couldn't reach the same wave to ride upon,
        kept wiping out discordantly
Her first aid kit filled with salt water and harmony
        so we could keep practising

She knew that no one could break my heart like you can
And no one could tape my heart like she could
Saying, don't worry darling, everyone knows tissue
        is stronger once it's been scarred
And you don't have to show the scars you have
        on your heart to everyone
But make sure you show them to this one, to the last love
Because she needs to see them
Needs to know when to be gentle, when to be hard
Needs to know when sentimentality is taking over you
So she can shake you and say: "Stop feeling sorry for yourself."

My mother bought that chocolate for you, too
Knew that no one could break your heart like I can
And if she could, she'd tape up your heart with tales
        that only a mother can tell
Anti-inflammatory tales, antiseptic tales that rooted in her mind
        and tumbled off her tongue, sprung from her lips
        to become stories that can heal you

And with each word sealing your wounds, you would know
      that there is nothing like a mother-in-law to tell you
      to tell me to stop feeling sorry for myself

My mother is sorry
Sorry that she couldn't be the one to tell you how proud we are
      to call you family
How proud she is of me to have been so smart to see that you
      were the one, the right one, the only one
You fit so perfectly- the sixth segment to our hexagon

You will try to know my mother
Draw her facial expressions like an artist on the canvas
      of your imagination
Compose her voice like a folk song in your mind
No, you'll never touch her hand, never hear her heart beat
      as she hugs you
But you will know my mother
I will make sure you were there, too
I will go back and superimpose you into the milestones of my life
The way that I've superimposed myself into the milestones of hers
Before I even began to exist as a maybe in my parents' minds
I touched her hands enough times to be able to pass that touch
      onto you through my touch
I have kept the memory of her skin

I will carve her fingerprints into driftwood and gift it to you
Ornament my love with her ideals for you
And when you ask I can show you how she smelt—I have it bottled,
      I wear her like a talisman on the nights I need her most

You have met my mother
I saw parts of me merging into parts of her long before I welcomed it
If you fell in love with my smile
You fell in love with hers
And her mother's before that
I have cherry picked bits of the best of her

171

Tried to shake bits of the worst of her

You have met my mother

My mother loves you
And you need to know that you're her daughter, too

I SLEPT IN THE MIDDLE
OF THE BED LAST NIGHT

I slept in the middle of the bed last night
And I know it doesn't sound like much
but the touch of the cold linen on the right was enough
        to bring her straight back to me

So I've been keen to leave that all behind
To step away, to redefine me

But every time the sun sets, it paints the sky with old memories
Candle-lit and underexposed
Sepia-stained and rust-burnt
and transports me to the first time we shared a bed

Or the day we didn't even try to get up
Because our legs were pinned down by each other's desire
Our arms weighted with each other's words
And our minds were so wrapped up in each other
        it would have taken hours to untangle ourselves
Even if we'd wanted to

And that day
It feels heady, and high, and I'm ready to open my mouth
        and take everything in, and my eyes
They're like newborn
Wedgwood saucers, with a pattern of gold leaf that catches
        every speck of light and bounces it back, reflected
        more brightly once meeting my gaze

And that day- we were tin men and rocking horses
Slipping in and out of character
Jesting and performing
Capering and cavorting

173

Our bodies were board games
Our hands were the tokens
And we were playing Monopoly on each other's skin

I was the shoe
In love with the idea that from tramping through
        the streets of London
Collecting property like football stickers
I could really become something

And she was the car
Because she said to me: "Baby, I'll take you to places
        you've never seen before
We'll take the high road travelling at high speed
        with the wind in our hair
High fiveing strangers without a care in the world
Because this is our kingdom
And in our infinite wisdom we're winsome and gleesome
And you and me, girl, we're the ultimate twosome."

And when we're finished with our high jinx we'll shift
        into gear and high tail it home
Ambitiously aimed arrows
70-mile-an-hour superheroes
And we'll fall into bed

And when we slept, I slept on the left
And her on the right
Even though each night she wanted to swap sides
Didn't want us to fall into rhythm
To slip into humdrum
Tear our hair out with boredom
We did

Because even in slumber we managed to disagree
And I needed air, I needed to breathe
While she cozied under the quilt

Tried to suffocate me
And the game played on

When we realised the money we had in our hands
        wouldn't buy us anything we needed at all
When it struck us that all it would take was a slip,
        was a fall and we were broken
The board was upended, the tokens gone flying,
        suspended in midair and someone's crying stop!
The rules have been changed!

Do not pass go, do not collect £200, and if you think
        that get out of jail free card you've been holding onto
        is valid in this game, think again

In this game, every roll you make lands you on a chance
In this game, every chance you take gets you a fine
In this game? Everyone loses

Because we'd been playing this game all wrong
We'd been building a house of cards out of our cards of streets
And it was fragile

These cards aren't even made to stand up this way
And as we climbed higher, we could feel it swaying
And the higher we climbed the further we had to fall

Anyway
I slept in the middle of the bed last night
It's been two months, almost three
And I've done some calculations
And if you type into Google how many days in 3 years it says 1095.73

1095.73 days spent together
395.679 nights spent living together
But to be honest, before that I slept in her bed so often
        I forgot the colour of my sheets

So I've heard that to get over someone it takes a person
        half as long as the length of the liaison
And that's—547.865 more sleeps
Minus 10 weeks
And that's—a really long time

But I'm taking it step by step, day by day, sleep by sleep, week by week
And this evening?
As I change out of my dressing gown
Turn down the sheets
Dim the lights
Wish myself sweet dreams

I might make a decision
Tonight? I'm going to sleep on the right

Nathan L W Hughes

Biography

Nathan L W Hughes is a native of Lincolnshire, a freelance writer/ script editor and winner of the East Midlands Under 25s Writers Challenge 2005. As writer-in-residence at Boston's Stump Radio (now Endeavour FM) he was head writer and devised their *Archers*-style audio soap opera, *The Mayflower*, which ran for two seasons between 2006 and 2008.

Outside of radio, Nathan has written for the Nottingham Playhouse, Theatre 503, E4, ITV Meridian and the Savvy Theatre Company. He is currently writing a children's musical for Heckington Youth Players and another for the Bunbury Banter Theatre Company's annual young theatre revue.

The Silver Separation

Dramatis personæ

CLIVE STANSFIELD
A male in his early seventies, balding and portly, speaks in a mild, northern twinged accent.

IRENA STANSFIELD
A female in her early seventies, short, nice hair, boring clothes, speaks with a well enunciated, home counties accent.

SCENE 1

Irena sits at a kitchen table in a simple kitchen. Atop the table are plates, utensiles, two mugs and various breakfast paraphernalia. Beside the table is a snug, two-seater sofa. Inoffensive, Radio 2-friendly music is faintly playing.

CLIVE *(off)*:

Good morning!

IRENA *(shouts as she butters toast)*:

Clive, you're letting all the heat out!

Clive enters, clutching a newspaper.

IRENA:

It's like Ice Station Zebra in here.

CLIVE:

I was collecting the paper.

IRENA:

Who were you talking to?

CLIVE:

Postman.

Clive takes a bundle of letters and bills from inside the newspaper. Irena ceases buttering her toast. Clive sits, places the newspaper on the table and opens a bill.

IRENA *(mild concern)*:

The post's early.

CLIVE:

He's a new chap, on the ball. Could you pass me the marmalade?

FX: Irena fidgets as Clive reads the bill.

CLIVE:
Phone bill's through the roof again, could you ring Mrs Mather after seven o'clock, when the calls are free?

IRENA *(relaxes)*:
I wouldn't want her to fall again, and she was a member of the drama society...

FX: Clive places the bill on the table, takes a sip from his mug and opens a letter.

CLIVE:
The marmalade please darling?

Clive scans the letter.

IRENA:
We've ran out.

Clive seizes up and drops his mug, which shatters on the floor. A beat before Irena pipes up.

IRENA:
I forgot to get any in the last shop.

Another beat. Clive continues reading the letter before slowly placing it on the table in front of him.

IRENA:
I'd better clean that up before the little ones arrive.

CLIVE *(mild shock, autospeak)*:
The marmalade?

IRENA *(gently)*:

Ran out...do you want to sit down?

CLIVE:

I'm sat down.

IRENA:

On the sofa.

CLIVE:

I'm quite all right here. I'd like to finish my toast. And since there's no marmalade, butter will have to suffice.

FX: *Clive grabs a round of toast and frantically butters it. He looses his grip on the knife and it clatters to the floor.*

CLIVE:

Did you not think to warn me in advance?

IRENA:

How?

CLIVE:

We spend almost twenty fours a day, seven days a week together, time enough I would have thought for us to have at least sat down, on the sofa, and discussed this in a calm and rational manner!

IRENA:

The two of us on the sofa, calm, collected and discussing this like adults is still an option. The toast's gone cold.

CLIVE:

Tough. I want to finish my tea. Is there another cup?

IRENA:

None that are clean.

CLIVE:

What about Tristan and Natasha?

IRENA:

What about them?

CLIVE:

Do they know?

IRENA:

They've...we've spoken.

CLIVE:

Oh excellent, so our children are in the loop?

IRENA:

I told them not to say anything.

CLIVE:

Who else knows? The grandchildren?

IRENA:

No.

CLIVE:

Mrs Mather?

IRENA:

Oh don't be ridiculous!

CLIVE:

It seems everyone and his dog is privy to this turn of events, everyone except me! Could you clean a cup for me?

IRENA:

Leave it.

CLIVE:

Fine, breakfast was turning into a washout anyway. Sofa?

They cross the room and relocate to the sofa, Clive taking the letter with him.

IRENA:

Anything interesting in the paper?

CLIVE:

Fuel strikes.

IRENA:

Unions again. This wouldn't have happened thirty years ago.

CLIVE:

But it's what I expect to be greeted with at breakfast, along with extortionate phone demands and junk mail, not divorce papers. I'm seventy-two years old...

IRENA:

...and I'm seventy-three.

IRENA:

It wasn't supposed to happen like this.

CLIVE:

So there was a plan?

IRENA:

I'd been waiting for the mail.

CLIVE:

So I could be kept even further in the dark...?

IRENA:

So I could read over what my solicitor had proposed and approach you with this properly.

CLIVE:

Scuppered by a postman who could actually be bothered to rise before eleven.

IRENA:

What do you want me to say?

CLIVE:

I want to know everything.

IRENA:

It's all there in the letter.

CLIVE:

The fine print doesn't interest me; I want to know how we've arrived at this point, where it all began.

IRENA (takes a breath):

Brittany.

CLIVE:

Was it someone on the campsite?

IRENA:

I don't understand?

CLIVE:

Did you meet a man on the campsite?

IRENA:

This has nothing to do with a man.

CLIVE:

Was it a valet boy?

IRENA:

No! We've been to that campsite every holiday, all August; the same pitch for as long as I can remember.

CLIVE:

And...?

IRENA:

It...I'm bored!

CLIVE:

Am I boring you?

Clive stands and begins to slowly pace the room.

IRENA:

Did I say that? That caravan, the same people...

CLIVE:

Calvin and Marie?

IRENA:

I can't face another summer of his anecdotes about the automotive industry and Marie...does that woman not know anyone with a life-threatening illness? It's not just them, it's the same outdoor pursuits, the same faces *(bordering on anger)* the same damn pitch!

CLIVE:

Then we'll spread our wings?

IRENA:

America, Australia, Iceland? I've always dreamt about a dip in the blue lagoon.

CLIVE:

That isn't fair; you know how I am with flying...

IRENA:

The same as I am with oversized spiders but I was willing to live the adventure!

CLIVE:

So this is what it's down to is it, my fear of air travel?

IRENA:

You don't have any fear, it comes from watching too many documentaries on the Discovery Channel...no Clive; this is the very tip, the section of the iceberg that isn't hidden underwater...

CLIVE:

Then enlighten me! I want to see the full iceberg, white, permafrosted and Titanic sinking in its might!

IRENA:

Would you like some cornflakes, before you surpass that embarrassingly accurate metaphor?

CLIVE:

I don't want anything...what I would like is deeper insight into why you've taken such drastic action concerning our marriage?

IRENA:

Clive, I...

CLIVE:

I don't want your indignation; we've gone over your dissatisfaction with our holidaying arrangements...

IRENA:

If you're looking for an inciting incident...

CLIVE:

I'm looking for answers to this *(waves letter)* breakfast time nasty that has landed on my lap.

IRENA *(sudden/sharp)*:

I don't like the script!

A beat.

CLIVE:
What exactly is wrong with the script?

IRENA:
May I?

Irena reaches down between the cushions of the sofa and pulls out a dog-eared, bound script.

IRENA *(opening the script)*:
That, that *(sifts through pages)* and that. I am not prepared to say such awful things about Mrs Thatcher on a public stage.

CLIVE:
The words belong to the character, not you!

IRENA:
They belong to a wet-behind-the-ears college dropout, who in November 1990 was probably still being bottle-fed!

CLIVE:
It's my job as drama society chairman to encourage new writing...

IRENA:
And turn us actors into cod socialist mouthpieces in the process? I wonder if a play entitled 'Milliband to the Gallows' would have been received with such gusto? No, you wouldn't allow a right-focused, left-bashing production to grace the boards, would you?

CLIVE *(protesting)*:
If it was well enough written I would! You've been blatantly obstructive in all society matters for as long as I can remember...you threw Ophelia right back in my face!

Irena stands and faces Clive.

IRENA:

Because I knew the second Clarissa Barnes walked through those doors you'd be casting her!

CLIVE *(protesting)*:

I cast on an actor's merit...

IRENA *(sarcasm)*:

Of course you do, age and the size of their bosoms having no bearing on your decision whatsoever!

CLIVE:

The committee and I cast her a team!

IRENA:

I would have thought you'd at least give me preference.

CLIVE:

I did, and the committee laughed. They were worried about accusations of nepotism if one of the leading ladies was sleeping with the director!

IRENA:

Well, no sleeping's gone on for nigh on a decade, so that was one worry the committee could have cast aside!

CLIVE:

Your reading was well below par...

IRENA:

Of course it was, with Clarissa's beady eye watching me.

CLIVE:

Ophelia was bidding farewell for what could be the last time, yet you sounded as if you were reeling off a takeaway order!

IRENA:

You weren't giving me any direction, because in your mind you'd already cast Clarissa Barnes!

CLIVE:

Well maybe I had. The drama society needed new, younger blood.

IRENA:

So you immediately gave up on me?

CLIVE:

I was hoping you'd up your game and not speak the words of Shakespeare as if they'd been written by Ronald McDonald.

CLIVE:

Clarissa was forty-two, from the perspective of the committee members that was younger blood.

Sighs. A beat. Clive throws himself down on the sofa.

IRENA:

Would you like me to put the kettle on?

CLIVE:

No.

IRENA:

We could have orange juice?

CLIVE:

We've still got a lot to talk about. A break would only affect the rhythm.

IRENA:

Now you're sounding like a director.

CLIVE:

I'll give you change Irena, if change is what you want. But seeking change by whatever means, even at the expense of a marriage that has been the bedrock of our family life, that has produced two exceptional children, two winners, is pointless.

Irena crosses over to the table and pours a glass of orange.

CLIVE:
I told you I didn't want a drink.

IRENA:
You need something to calm you down.

CLIVE:
I do indeed and the liquid required won't be found in an orange juice carton.

Irena returns to the sofa, sits, and hands the orange juice to Clive.

CLIVE:
So let me get this right, not casting you in Hamlet, the staging of a challenging piece of theatre and a perfectly rational dislike of flying have lead to *(raises the letter)* this?

IRENA:
You've missed out Clarissa Barnes.

CLIVE:
The youngest person to join the drama society in years, idealistic, ambitious...she gave her all as Ophelia...

IRENA:
Despite being twenty years too old for the part and measuring in at six feet two?

CLIVE:
When Clarissa proposed a musical about the life of Margaret

Thatcher, I was already bowled over by her commitment, her charisma, so of course I was going to agree to it. I still don't see what bearing she has on all this?

IRENA:
A lot. And Silas helped make the decision.

CLIVE:
Our two-year-old grandson? Last time I asked he wanted to be an astronaut, not a lawyer.

IRENA:
He couldn't tell his toys apart from Clarissa's jewellery...of course he was going to play with it. I can't guess as to how long it was lodged behind the sofa. Has the penny dropped Clive, have you made two and two?

CLIVE *(shocked/stammers)*:
It...that is no reason to jump straight into a divorce!

IRENA:
A husband cheating on his wife? The courts'll see that as pretty standard.

CLIVE:
Couldn't you have told me?

IRENA *(surprise/indignation)*:
Couldn't you have told me?!

CLIVE:
Of course I couldn't. You didn't suspect a thing, and what you didn't know wouldn't hurt you. Darling, I...

IRENA:
...believed our marriage to be stable, to be routine enough to withstand a clandestine affair?

CLIVE:

But we have a connection. We do things together—everything together—Provence, the Scottish Play, Rocky Horror, Bruges...?

IRENA:

But not enough it seems, otherwise you wouldn't have Clarissa filling in the gaps.

Clive exhales hard, unsure of how to respond.

IRENA:

How was she for you?

CLIVE:

I'm not answering that...I thought you'd be above those who demand to know every detail...hang on a tick, for me?

IRENA:

For you.

CLIVE:

Are you implying there have been others?

IRENA:

Any one of the all-male drama society committee, you'd never know, would you?

CLIVE:

My God, I never thought...

IRENA:

...that Clarissa would be satisfied with just you?

CLIVE *(horrified)*:

Oh my God! But I've known some of those men for years, I know where they've been...Soho, ladies of the night, French letters strewn far and wide across a boardroom table...I could have picked up anything! I mean, all the trouble I've been having with my waterworks...?

IRENA:

...but surely it's better not to know? You wouldn't suspect a thing, and surely what you didn't know couldn't hurt you?

CLIVE *(horrified)*:

Are the doctors open on a Saturday? You know Irena...were the shoe on the other foot, I would have understood you know. I would have turned a blind eye.

Clive raises the orange juice and drinks.

IRENA:

Of course you would, it would have alleviated your own sense of guilt. So when I had my affair *(Clive spits out the juice, spraying Irena, who proceeds to wipe it daintily from her face and clothes)*, I thought it best if I were discreet about it.

Clive wipes the juice from his mouth, which is agog with surprise.

IRENA:

Don't you want to know who they are? What position we did it in? Don't you want to set off on a pointless mission to kill 'them', to show off some masculine integrity?

CLIVE:

But...but...?

IRENA:

No buts, its OK, you said yourself you'd understand.

CLIVE:

It's a different ball game, didn't you stop to think about danger, what about pregnancy?

IRENA:

193

At my age?

CLIVE:
It didn't stop the *Star Trek* chap...and sexually transmitted ailments, have you thought about those? H...HIV for instance?

IRENA:
Not a problem either.

CLIVE:
How?

IRENA:
The blind eye is still an option.

CLIVE:
It's gone beyond that now, if we have any hope of salvaging our marriage then perhaps, against my better judgement, we'd benefit from being completely honest with one other.

Clive stands, mops his brow and turns away from Irena.

CLIVE *(deep breath)*:
I regret to inform you that for the past six months, I have been *(embarrassment)* getting to know Clarissa Barnes *(he turns back to Irena)*. Your turn.

IRENA:
I regret to inform you that for the past six months, I have been getting to know Clarissa Barnes.

CLIVE:
That's what I said, I'm not proud of it but if there's any chance it'll make a difference, I'm prepared to bare the truth.

IRENA:
I have been getting to know Clarissa Barnes.

CLIVE:

I know the honest truth is difficult to hear, but I've said my piece, now I think you should say yours...

IRENA:

I've been getting to know Clarissa Barnes, intimately.

CLIVE:

We've already gone over that Irena...

IRENA (FIRM):

I have been screwing Clarissa Barnes!

CLIVE:

I heard you...(A BEAT, REALITY SINKS IN) Oh!

IRENA:

I told you from the start it had nothing to do with a man.

CLIVE:

But...she stole Ophelia from you!

IRENA:

I know. It hurt, but everyone only ever saw Clarissa and I as rivals. The perfect smokescreen.

CLIVE:

She meant nothing to me. Whatever pleasure I derived from the situation was overshadowed in bulk by guilt.

IRENA:

I just needed someone...someone who fully understood what it is a woman wants...

CLIVE:

And who better to find that from than another woman?

IRENA:

Clarissa was my first...and she will be my last.

CLIVE:

It's far too soon to try and draw a line under this...

IRENA:

Not for me it isn't.

CLIVE:

Why?

IRENA:

Clarissa was very selfish. I'm no closer to discovering what I really want than I was before.

CLIVE:

So what will you do?

IRENA:

I don't know. Right now all I can think of is the little ones arriving any minute now.

CLIVE:

Do you want me to make their breakfast?

IRENA:

I will...

CLIVE:

Let's do it together.

A brief silence as Irena rises, crosses over to the table and begins clearing it. Suddenly Clive pipes up.

CLIVE:

Did the lip 'thing' bother you?

IRENA:

I had noticed.

CLIVE:

...me too, on more than one occasion I subtly mentioned 'upper lip hair removal' to her. You can have it on the state these days.

IRENA:

I didn't go that far, I just asked if she'd ever heard of Immac.

Irena piles plates and utensiles into Clive's arms.

IRENA:

It was Clarissa's pillow talk that bothered me. Did she mention her next project?

CLIVE:

'Nick Clegg in the Underworld?'

IRENA:

That's the one.

CLIVE:

I told her not to bother with a sequel...

IRENA:

Spare a thought for me. I'm up for the part of his wife...I've no idea how to politely decline.

CLIVE:

That's easy: tell her you're sleeping with the director.

Cautious laughter from Irena and Clive as they exit.

END

NIK WAY

BIOGRAPHY

Nik writes, acts and directs, occasionally doing some work for his degree. He has been known to shave his head for a part and undress during poetry readings. In 2013 he was shortlisted for the Young Poet Laureate of London. He is currently a member of the Roundhouse Poetry Collective 2014/15. *Broadway Baby* described his play *Last Supper* as 'thought-provoking and poignant'. He (barely ever) maintains a blog at nikofway.wordpress.com and (fairly frequently) tweets from @NikWay.

JUNK

That shirt I wore to prom
no longer fits.
It sits inside the box
stuffed with sleeves and socks.

It spotted me when shopping,
showed its stripes and cut
a hard bargain,
You buy me
I beautify you.

It hung smug in my closet,
never let my school-shirts forget
when a guy called it fly at a party
before it met his jeans on the floor

It was speechless the day it saw snow,
after it fell in a drift it choked up and cried.
It dried, but it was never quite
the shirt it had been.

It took to solitude, watched
the oldest closet-lodger
it used to look down on,
covered in signatures scrawled by children
asking to keep in touch, kick me,
get packed away in the loft above my bed.

It was dropped
on top of a soft soiled vest
quite beneath it.

It pleaded in the car,
I am worthy
see my stripes!
Words muffled
by the cardboard box.

It may have been screaming
when I dropped it off
but I didn't hear it.

FRIEND

I liked your picture
at the beach in your frock-coat.
Greyscale suits your antique looks.
Remember when you borrowed
my felt fedora?

I see you snapped in clubs:
damp, arms folding around
a girl pushing herself
toward your full lips.

You tried to delete our pictures
but I installed a copy in my soul
of the night your hand wandered.
I still feel phantom fingers around me
when all the lights go out.

I watch you walk down the street,
sharing earbuds with a new girl,
wonder if I took her place
you'd notice me slotting into your waist,
head on shoulder
as the song shuffled onto The Killers.

ODE TO THE MAN IN THE GYM

You are to grasp the handles
and with all the might you can muster,
push down.

He doesn't.
He sits and stares at
those women on the stepper
or the man heaving half his weight
above his head, sweat creating damp patches
in mysterious patterns that get you wondering
about the lay lines of the male torso.

Meanwhile the sitter sips
at his bottled water, shifts in his
throne of lethargy, ignoring dirty looks
from the impatient.

Does he sit in a restaurant like this?
Ordering nothing—watching, sipping, sitting,
staring at the waiter when he comes until he goes.
Is his lovemaking motionless? Is the only reason for walking
to find another place to rest his rear?

Like a child who doesn't understand musical chairs,
guarding his like a fortress, only skimming to another
when sure it won't get stolen in the intervening seconds.
Moving through the world via a network of
chairs and benches and stools.
Until he comes to a river and the only way across
to the seat on the far side is to take a dive
and plunge into the unknown.

HOMETOWN

Just another glass tipped,
chinking against his teeth.
Just another night spent
out, in regular haunts
where they know what he wants
before the door behind him closes.
Just another boy
who will go home in an hour
or two to the bedroom he was born in
twenty-one years ago.

He's happy as the goldfish
he barely feeds.
At night he no longer sees
the domed glass sky
covering hometown like a snow globe.

He knows who he is.
If only his friends could be so sure;
they flitted away to find themselves.
He had to buy an address book
and the list of those to meet, chat, fuck
recedes with his hair.

I went back.

He couldn't hear me when I spoke of anything
that fell beyond hometown's glass wall,
didn't believe there was a world outside,
urged me to stay
like in the old days,
relive the times we had,
return to my roots.

I hefted a hammer and slammed
the weight against the glass.
Not even a crack.

I could take the globe and turn it upside down,
shake people from their homes,
squirrels from uprooted trees,
swirl it all in a whirligig
of unrest and confusion.
Returning hometown upright,
everything would settle
in much the same place as before.

INK

White hair in curlers
faded lipstick and greening tattoos
her nails no longer match
her eyes, milky and unfocused.

She inhales, smiles,
exhales and laughs.
Dust stirred by the door
settling.

I offer her a cup of still water.
She pulls me over, her piercing
scratches my cheek.
She plants her lips on my jaw
and empties a sleeve, shows me

the inky girl on her shoulder
sipping scotch in a summer field
surrounded by flowery boys
smoking green pipes, ushering in
a new age with guns
made of guitar strings and a pocketful
of infectiously happy plants.

I brush the girl's face
the woman's shoulder
with my fingertip.
She strums a chord
that fells the king of Jericho
bakes me a cake like I've never had
from a recipe long forgotten
undresses
me first
then slowly
breaks her necklace, beads
rolling in circles around her bare feet.

Later I considered
getting a tattoo of two of us
in her bath
on my chest
but knew the artist
couldn't capture her green eyes
that stare at me still
when I fall asleep.

DREAMCATCH

Pouring through old boxes
like an urban fox, I found
a dusty dreamcatcher.

It sang, little sparks falling from it.
A daydream darted out, full of fun
it zoomed around the room and fancied itself
driving a rally over the craters of the moon.

A pipedream appeared, prouder
than the last, it stomped around,
but lost its gusto when the sun set.
It's taken to hiding under the bed,
so no one can see it unfulfilled.

A few more tumbled out, but there was one stuck
its foot was caught between a bead and string.

It's the one where I was too big for my room
and the house was my cage. I awoke in a sweat,
clinging to my normal-size teddy.

I let the nightmare grasp my finger
hoisted it away from the trap,
held it close, then let it free.
'No hard feelings' I said. But it wasn't listening,
it was too busy dancing its first dance for years.

SHOW US

An unwanted mirror stands vigil
on the kerb, snatching
portraits of passersby who
take no notice

I check myself daily
in that lonesome silver sheet.
Can mirrors have memories?

Sometimes, there's a pigtailed girl
in the corner or
the stern eyes of her father
staring over my shoulder

On Fridays it plays games; puts
a bowler or red curls on my head, makes me
fat, tall, beautiful

Last weekend it was spent, too tired
by the wash of people
unconcerned by their reflection
too reveal any untruth

I looked at it
It looked at me and peeled back
the glass, unveiling its wish
to become a gold-framed
oil painting of two tigers
photographing the caged hunter with
mirth in their amber eyes.

UNITED KINGDOM OF AMERICA

I was born one September,
read the Magna Carter and the Sun,
learnt to argue with foreigners on the Tube.
I packed my encyclopaedias and flew
across the Atlantic.

Air tastes different here.
Settlers must have bombed
the plains with pine-forest perfume
to force the Indians out.

My translator meets me at the airport
and drives me through the Midwest
on the tear-stained trail of a murderous stag.

I'm given a gun on the hunt
but refuse, taking a white feather instead.
He enjoys my cowardice and we track a diner
where shakes are tall and frothy, where
waitresses grin with neon teeth.

Over a platter of red-meat shipped from overseas
he petitions my government to
get their shit together and join the just
cause for bloodshed in the dark
places of the world.
I reach for my feather but
the rare steak glistens.

I ask about the stag.
He says they let it stay in an exclusive hotel,
dressed it in a fine orange tux
and sat it on a high-tech chair
when it solved my problem with strangers on the Tube
before unfortunately checking out.

My friend slips the stag's solution
into my shirt pocket and winks.

The bill arrives, steeper than expected,
we agree to split the cost between
two of our mutual friends, promising
to reimburse them in later years.
While we're at it, add one wine and a root beer.
We may as well be merry as we dance
our way into oblivion.

HELLO

Those first sounds a foreign tongue makes
in your mouth. A parcel exchanged between
old friends in the arrivals lounge, wrapped in a smile
with both arms pressing close.

Others learnt to sign: a head that nods
to fellow truckers, bobbing along the highway
at seventy miles an hour.

An extended hand. The duel:
who shakes first, who grips hardest.
Battle becomes war
collateral damage of palms slapping
arms and backs.

Dogs know their stuff: size them up, snarl,
sniff in infinite circles of fur and noses
while their owners laugh, apologise and discuss
this bloody weather we've been having.

Sinead Cooper

Biography

Sinéad Cooper moved from London to Liverpool in 2011, and graduated from Liverpool John Moore's University in 2014 with a BA in Creative Writing. As part of The Wild Writers she has built a poetry vending machine, and shaved her head while performing her poem 'Reactions to a Bald Woman'. In 2013, she was longlisted for the Bridport Prize with her poem 'Bedtime Rituals'.

Bedtime Rituals

She sits on our bed,
Its duvet spotted with wine
and cigarette burns,
reaches her thick arms around
to unhook her bra,
loop the straps off her shoulders:
she bares an imprint
cooling on her back.
Scored red lines
curve round under her breasts.
Two pink dents run
fading over each shoulder.

As she leans forward
to pull off odd socks,
I count the notches of her spine.
She stretches her arms up
rolls her head,
and I count the clicks of her bones,
the crickling in her neck and wrists.
She slumps back,
sinks into our tangled bed,
where I count the colours of her tattoo
stamped at her pelvis for an ex-husband.
She rolls to her side,
lies her rough hand on mine,
I count the creases of her palm
running over my knuckles—

We lie together and I count
in dim lamp light, I wonder
at the tired end of another day,
if her husband ever found the same numbers,
ever noticed these same marks.
If any man could see the same lines
as I do.

I WISH WEED WAS REAL

and alcohol imagined
when I'm cocooned in sheets,
hidden from the dying sun
of another missed day
and you're dribbling nonsense
through zeroes and ones
and ones and zeroes
I still feel the weight of the night before,
the 6am key in the lock
pressing a film of pub filth on my skin.

Ring me at midnight
when my blood's clean
and my skin sober.
Convince me the party was made up
and we'll share the reality of this joint.

HIDDEN

Magda typed away, her fingers tapping the keys fast while her eyes stayed fixed on the old boxy monitor. It glared a soft blue on her face and reflected white squares in her glasses. Her desk was covered in manila folders in short piles about the keyboard and monitor. One folder lay open on top of a pile to Magda's left. Now and then, without pausing, she glanced at it, or in one smooth, quick movement, she turned a page while one hand moved across the keys. The only space clear of files was to her right, room for the mouse, and behind the monitor where the desk turned into an all-purpose table where there sat two unfinished mugs of tea.

The room was large, carpeted green, except for a patch of white lino where the basic kitchen was squashed in a corner. There was a squat two-person sofa and an old TV facing it, three filing cabinets against a wall, three wooden chairs, a messily filled bookcase, and one wide window currently covered by heavy olive curtains. Along with the clack of Magda's typing, the computer hummed, a clock ticked above the door, and there were muffled thumps from outside as Leila made her way up the flat's stairs. Magda stood up as Leila walked through the door. Magda picked up the mugs and went to the kitchen corner, where she rinsed them and placed them next to the kettle.

'*Another* eyelash.' Leila slumped onto the sofa, fleece zipped up to her chin and satchel over her shoulder. 'Or hair, finger smudge, dust, whatever.'

Magda hummed an 'uh huh' as she filled the kettle at the sink, tilting it at an awkward angle to avoid the ever-collecting pile of washing up.

Leila kicked at the heels of her boots. 'I mean, how many times is it now that I've had to tell someone *sorry, no ghost here, just give your camera lens a wipe,*' she groaned when her boots wouldn't come off, leaning forward to pull at the laces. 'And this guy, he wouldn't believe me, just insisted there must be a ghost in his spare room.' Leila pulled off her boots and chucked them. They landed next to a stack of The Anomalist back issues leant against the bookcase. 'So, of course, I had to do a photo reconstruction, and he still wouldn't believe me.'

217

She reclined into the sofa, pulled her satchel strap over her head, and unzipped her fleece. 'His photo and mine looked exactly the same, but he's in total denial!'

Magda waited by the kettle, teabags and sugar in the mugs. 'You don't have to do a reconstruction every time,' Magda's voice was flat as ever. 'Some people are too stubborn to-'

'Believe the evidence? Hm, sounds like someone I know,' Leila grinned and brought her hand to her chin in a mock-thinking pose

The kettle clicked as it reached a boil, steam puffed to the cupboard above it, where the white laminate was crinkled and yellowed. Magda's brow creased into a faint frown. 'There's a difference between hard evidence and your wild theories for simple anomalies.' She poured the kettle.

'Come on, stop saying that all the time. There's nothing simple about the weird stuff we've seen. What about that werewolf in Croydon?'

Magda brought the teas over to the couch. A cartoon alien was printed on one mug, with large bug eyes and a Hawaiian shirt. The other was plain blue. 'I told you, I only saw it for a second. It looked like a very big and startled dog to me.' She sat on the couch's arm.

Leila laughed, reached an arm up and flicked Magda in the forehead. 'That's why you shouldn't buy your glasses from a rack in Poundland' She took the alien mug and sipped. 'Anyway, what about Paul? Noting simple there either.' Leila stopped mid-sip, a thought catching her. 'Looked simple though. Standing outside that dead-end house, waving his phone around and shouting to me.'

Magda's face went blank, her lips a flat line, her brow smoothed from any expression.

'And then he wasn't standing there, wasn't there at all. Pinched from existence. Simple as that.'

'He'll be somewhere. He still exists.'

'Does he? There's no answer to his phone. He's not in his flat, not at his mum's, he's hasn't come back here. We've checked that house and every road near it. We've walked all over Ealing and Harrow. He's nowhere.' Leila stood up sharply, some tea splashing onto the carpet. 'If you saw it Mags, saw him vanish right there, you'd get it.' Leila went to the kitchen, left her mug on the desk.

Magda nodded. 'I get it. Wild theories are all we've got.'

Leila opened the fridge door, scanning inside for a meal to throw together. Her phone buzzed in her pocket and gave off a wood pigeon coo.

'A new case?' Magda asked.

'Hopefully,' Leila brought out her phone. There were scratches over its back and one fine crack running diagonally over the screen. The room's bare bulb highlighted smudges all over the glass in white.

'I hope it's a UFO. All these ghost photos are getting boring.' It had been a while since Magda had investigated a ghost case, or any case. She preferred working at the computer.

'This is ghost country, Mags. It's the old buildings and all those dead knights and earls everywhere,' Leila tapped and swiped at her phone screen with her thumb, her nail bitten short. 'You can't escape it, you know, the layers of history everything's built on.' She paused to read the email she had just received. Her eyebrows raised, she slammed the fridge shut. 'It's Paul!'

'What?'

'Paul! He's emailed me.'

'What? What has he said? Is he ok?'

The phone trembled in Leila's hand. 'I don't know. All he's said is Meet at the top of Regents Close. Read file #224 on the way.'

Magda half stood. A nauseous excitement hit her stomach and she sat back down. 'It's on the desk.' She nodded her head to the open file she read from earlier.

'You were typing it up today?'

'Yeah. File #224, Regents Close'

Leila had rushed to the desk. She closed the file and opened it again at the first page.

Magda's back straightened and she spoke quietly, almost to herself. 'I had just gotten to the section on Paul's disappearance.'

Leila snapped the folder shut again. Her face was manic. 'Spooky.' She zipped up her fleece and checked the clock. 'You were right, he still exists. Here's the proof.' She passed her phone to Magda and picked up her boots. 'Come on, we don't want him to vanish again.'

*

They were standing at the top of Regents Close, waiting by a garden wall on the corner. Magda leant against it with her gloved hands in her pockets. Leila stood straight, staring down the cul-de-sac to its dead end. It had taken them over an hour to get from Brent to Ealing. They had stood the whole journey, the tube busy and stuffy from the rush hour, the bus they got from Ealing Broadway was packed with school children. When they had reached Regents Close, Leila began to walk down it before Magda stopped her and insisted they stay at the top, just as Paul's email said. They had now been waiting on the corner of the cul-desac for almost two hours. They killed the first hour going over File #224, its corners bent and creased from being shoved into Leila's satchel.

Magda turned to the house the wall belonged to. The garden was neat and plain, only a square patch of even lawn. A curtain twitched on the first floor. A few seconds later a light switched on in a small downstairs window. 'Leila, we should move. Someone will think we're up to something suspicious.'

'We'll cross the road then.' She stepped off the curb between two parked cars.

'And wait on someone else's garden wall for another two hours?'

Leila crossed to the house opposite. 'He's late, always is.'

Magda followed. 'Late? He didn't even give us a time. Are we meant to wait here all night? All week?'

'What else are we meant to do? That email is all we've got.' Leila sat on the wall opposite one of the birch trees that lined the road, their spindly trunks reaching from grass squares in the pavement. Street lamps beside them stretched higher to the blank sky, shining an orange haze on the cars and wheelie bins parked by the kerb. A light turned on in a window of the dead-end house. A plain empty room was illuminated for a moment in its curtain free glass, before the light flickered off.

Leila jumped up, eyes wide. 'Did you see that?' She ran into the road and sprinted down Regents Close, boots slapping on the tarmac.

'What?' Magda jogged after her.

'That light. It was the same me and Paul saw,' Leila shouted back, her phone held up in front of her.

'Wait, Leila, we should stay up here.' Nausea hit Magda again, no excitement this time, only anxiety swirled in her stomach.

Leila stopped at the rusted garden gate to the dead-end house. She took a few pictures with her phone. 'I need proof Mags. I need to know what it is.'

'It?' Magda had caught up and stood just behind Leila's shoulder. She breathed hard, hand on the stich that twanged just under her ribs.

'The house. This cul-de-sac. Whatever it is that's been vanishing people.'

'We only know for sure about Paul's disappearance. And even then-'

'Do you read those files at all when you type them up?' Leila started filming, she moved the phone's view over the house and down its garden path.

'Yes. I know what you're getting at, but no one witnessed the others like you saw Paul.' Magda crossed her arms, squinted her eyes at the house. The garden was bare mud, scattered with faded crisp packets, dented beer cans, ripped plastic bags. Rubbish blown over the low wall or through the gate leant open on one hinge. 'Sometimes people just go missing. It's how cities work.' She waved her hand to the street behind them. 'There's too many places to hide, or be hidden.'

Leila stepped towards the gate, put a hand on its flaking black bars.

Magda pulled her back by the shoulder. 'Wait.'

Leila stumbled. 'Let go.' She pulled away.

Magda chewed her top lip, the rest of her face still and plain.

'Look, maybe you're right. All these homes, all their doors, we don't know what's behind them. Maybe Paul's hiding, maybe he's hidden in that house now.' Leila stepped through the gate.

'Wait!' Both women jumped round to the shout behind them. Paul ran down Regents Close, his unfastened parka jacket flapped and its hood bobbed on his head.

'Paul?' Leila's face scrunched.

'Wait, get out of there!' His eyes were wide and red.

Leila kicked the gate, it fell off the wall with a clatter. 'Where the hell have you been?'

'Forget about it, just get out!'

The panic in Paul's voice made Magda's mind scramble, only one thought stuck out. She swivelled, a knee bent to leap over the broken gate and yank Leila out. She halted. Leila wasn't there.

'Magda, don't.' Paul shoved her away. She crashed into a birch tree, its branches rattled together. 'I've been where she's going.'

He vaulted over the wall, swinging his legs over, one hand on the brick. The mud made a splat when he landed, then vanished. Magda wobbled to the wall, knelt a leg on it and searched where the garden met the bottom of the wall. She hoped he had fell, that he would be crouched against the wall clutching a grazed hand or bruised knee. He wasn't.

She got back off the wall and walked to the garden's entrance. Nothing. She hesitated at the threshold, where the pavement joined with the worn mud of the garden path. She closed her eyes tight, her nostrils flared. She took a step into the garden towards the house. She waited. A dog barked in someone's garden far away. She opened her eyes, rimmed with the beginning of tears. The house stared her own, its windows dark and blank.

Magda followed the path to the side of the house. The front door, wooden and peeling white paint, was ajar. She pushed it open. Her and Leila checked the house twice when Paul had disappeared. Nothing strange, other than how empty it was. A bulb above the doorway lit up, it flickered and buzzed. Magda rested a hand on the door frame and swallowed hard. The bulb popped, the hallway was blacked out again.

Magda twisted and ran out into the road, down Regents Close and around the corner past endless front lawns and lampposts. She ran until she reached the main road, busy with traffic and a bright shopping parade. She rested against the glass of a fish and chip shop. Inside, a man knocked on the glass, scowled and pointed for her to get off. She waited at the bus stop. A stitch dug again at her side, her mouth was dry. A group of teenagers sniggered and an elderly couple stared as she wheezed for breath. She wished she could disappear back to the flat, walk through the door and find Leila on the coach, still drinking her tea.

Kat Day

Biography

Kat Day is a 20-something queer writer from Leeds. She has been writing poetry for 10 years and recently started performing it. Some of the following poems appear online in the digital collection *Athena was Not Jealous.*

ATHENA WAS NOT JEALOUS
A sequence

1. AMPHITRITE

I curled inside myself,
Bit my tongue and
Forgot the lessons
They taught me, but
No more.

I have oceans beneath my flesh,
Roaring with the sounds of
Lost civilisation and
I could not be quiet if
You begged me.

Listen,
For I am Earth and Air
And holy Fire, sent to
Cleanse your violence
With something so fierce it
Burns.

I am alive,
And I am bigger than
Every load you thrust upon my back.
I shall not carry your burdens.
I shall break them.

2. WANDERLUST

I am homesick,
But not for home.
There are places I have never been
And yet, I miss them terribly.
There's a whole world that
I've never seen, but
My soul screams to experience and
I think that's my cue.

One day, my feet will touch
Red sand and
Black beaches and
Mountain tops.
I will absorb oceans and hurricanes
And build myself so strong that
You can find the universe in my eyes.

Maybe then, I will
Find you.

3. LOVE

I want to climb inside your skin,
Make a home in your brain,
And listen.

I want to know more about you than anyone,
To predict what you'll say,
But to listen regardless,
Because I love the way you say it.

I want to understand,
To feel each line on your skin,
And scar on the walls of your heart,
And to know the stories that made them.

I want to know you so well,
That sometimes we forget we're two people,
When it's late,
And we're awake,
More comfortable together
Than we are in our own flesh.

Let me in. Let me wear you.
Let me know what it's like to suffer your downs,
And ride your ups,
And I'll show you my wounds,
And expose to you my thoughts,
Until we know each other
Better than we know ourselves.

4. QUEER

The first time I heard the word
Lesbian,
I was 8 years old and
They came from lips I'd just kissed.

I thought it was swearing,
That if her mother
Had heard her say it
She would be grounded for a week.

When it sits in my mouth,
It still feels heavy,
And my stomach churns the way it did
When I skipped class.

I'm not the only one who,
Growing up,
Thought sexuality was insulting,
And struggled to find myself there,

But I still feel lost,
And sometimes I'm convinced that
The words I think are the worst
Are the ones which fit best.

5. BROTHER

My hands are small
Like my shoulders and
As I fold inwards,
I repeat training.

It was never said aloud,
But we were taught to be
Reactive
And taking up less space is
Safer than demanding a voice.

Now, I shout so loud I
Wake up hungover with
A throat so sore I can't
Make noise,
Yet still, you don't listen.

Instead,
You say that one day,
I'll grow up from my
Rebellion.

All I can hear is
'*One day we'll break you.*'

That's *threat*,
Not reassurance.

6. BINDING

I have been uncomfortable in my own skin for

14 years
      7 months
           and 2 days.

         It was my seventh birthday and,
        upon opening my presents,
        all bright eyes and
        childish excitement,

                    I found a bra.

        It was a small thing.

                Frilly.

        Pink polka dots and
   white lace
        and I,
        ever polite,
                smiled through my tears.

Last month my mother stood as a statue while
I cried in the bathroom for over an hour,

        because my chest was infected
        and the doctor would have to

                remove my only armour to
                expose my back to cold steel.

And my mother *(because she's the type of person
who irons her clothes before she packs them
to travel across the globe)*,

could not bear to see me wear a bra that was not
'pretty'.

So, purple satin, push up, plunge neckline
restraints were strapped to me,

and I could not find a jumper baggy enough.

Yesterday, you said that my outfit makes me look
like a 15 year old boy.

I said, *That's why I like it.*

You might not appreciate that
some days I want to step outside myself,

but don't tell me I'm strange for idolising bodies
that are more pleasing than my own.

You do that,

too.

Rei Haberberg

Biography

Rei lives in London with too many people and not enough cats. They overthink most aspects of daily life, which is where they get ideas for fiction, and of popular culture, which is where they get ideas for non-fiction—they can be found blogging about romance novels at Bad Reputation in their spare time. Someday Rei hopes to be able to hire somebody to write biographies for them.

As I Ought to Be

First appeared in [no definition], *Lent 2012 issue.*

You might see him at the theatre—although he looks so out of place there it's ludicrous, in a velvet frock coat over torn and faded jeans. People ask about his outfits a lot, and he never has an answer, his fashion sense as contrary as a bus timetable; the only constants about his clothing are the cowboy boots, the brown leather scuffed and scarred with age, and the hat. In bars and cafes he might be seen with any number of people, but for concerts and conventions he seems to have a companion picked out for each, and for the theatre it's a slender man with a fine-boned face and suits so sharp you're almost afraid of the edges. They have a box of their own, it would seem, and during intervals they'll stand next to each other and talk soft and easy, heads bowed, gazes drifting around the room. Together, they look just incongruous enough to blend in.

You'll see her on horseback, although not so much in the city, and wonder why she never puts up her hair. There've been sightings of elastic, some say, tangled in the thick dark mass of it, but whether she's tried to keep it away or not it's down around her shoulders and over her face by the time you run across her, and it's hard to see how she keeps on course. Sometimes she lets the beast amble her around town and doesn't seem to care much where she goes and sometimes you'll see her one minute and the next she's off towards the desert and picking up speed, dark eyes flashing, now and again with some laughing girl giving chase. Best not to stare after 'em too long, or the sand'll get in your eyes.

Or you'll see them in a bar, and they might be wearing any old thing; it's oddest when they're in a shirt and some kind of corsetry, for the fall and crease of the linen lies smooth in some places and in others makes curves of what might be flat planes and angles. They might be in the thick of things, playing pool or at the hub of some joke or a brewing fight, sitting at a lady's feet or with a gentleman on their arm, or just by themselves, sprawled loose-limbed with a pipe or a fag or one of them other things, the long slender cigarettes they put in a holder to smoke. (If you look carefully you might see them try to blow a smoke ring, but that's not often and it never happens by chance; they never really mastered the trick, you see, and the only way you'd be able to watch long enough to see 'em muck it up would be to keep your eyes fixed at all times, and that's the sort of thing that people notice.)

Sometimes he's out-loud and showy, striding around town at midday in an evening dress with feathers in his hair, and sometimes he's just some scruffy lanky boy at the bus stop, too young to be wise, too grown-up to be awkward. Sometimes she's all white cotton skirts over those scuffed-up cowboy boots and sometimes she's in overalls, spotless ones, sharp and bright against her sun-browned sandy skin. They'll have the hat on, like as not, looking like it's fighting a losing battle with that thick dark hair but somehow staying on regardless; or if it's not on their head it's somewhere about them, tucked under one arm, slung carelessly over one shoulder.

Often you'll be in conversation with her before you even realise it. He's a decent enough talker, after all, and if you're by yourself in a dark room and the air's misted with smoke and your brain's fuzzed over with beer, you'll be drawn into the conversation before you remember what you're supposed to be looking out for. She seems to like it that way; it draws the wariness out of her eyes, the ever-present don't mess with me hint that lurks behind his smile whenever they're somewhere they're not sure is safe. There're layers on layers in that smile, and the surface one's the same as the very deepest, which you'd think would make him an easy type but actually makes him tricky to talk to, sometimes, especially when you're asking all the wrong questions. Then they look at you like you're missing the point, somehow, like you're not getting the joke. (It's okay; you're not the first, and you won't be the last. It's obvious once you've figured it out, but sometimes that takes time, like the really good restaurant that everyone's heard of but that's only ever half-full 'cause the route's not the clearest and you'll get lost on the way there unless you already know where it is.)

Some people wonder why it's funny. She can get them quite worked up about it, if she's in the right sort of mood.

You know them, though, because everybody does, even if not all of them seem to get it either. Some people figure it out and some don't; the ones who know or don't care don't need to ask, and some people never get much further than wanting to know, because it seems rude to bring it up. You might be one of those, and that's natural enough; it's the kind of thing you might expect people to be offended about if it's talked about, after all, if it's brought out into the open.

Not everybody's as polite as you, though, and it's only a matter of time before you see that too; that one person who, out of malice or curiosity or just plain confusion, leans in at the bar or barges through the crowd in the shopping mall or just plain sees her, stops, looks him up and down, and takes the long or the short way round to that big question: 'What are you?'

You might miss it; it's normally over quicker than you'd expect, after all, the eyebrow raise where you'd expect shock, the grin or chuckle where you'd think to find an awkward silence.

They'll tip their head back, and smile, and wink. 'I am exactly as I ought to be, darlin',' they'll say.

It's the only answer they can give, because it's the only answer there is.

They're exactly as they ought to be.

That's the only answer that matters.

A Scream in Diamond

'There's an alligator in the middle of the kitchen floor.'

He has to wonder about this as she says it, because there's no inflection in her voice; if she finds the strange, reptilian presence in their home unusual or disturbing in any way, she certainly isn't showing it, but neither does she appear amused or even interested by it.

Unusual, for her. Or it used to be.

Less unusual is that she's come to wake him up at four in the morning and found him already awake. They still sleep in the same room, sometimes—there's been no formal move there—but the moments when she doesn't want anyone around her come more and more often these days, and he knows, and knows that she knows he knows but doesn't want to upset him; so he works late and sleeps in the living room, more often than not, so that she can come to find him if something scares her without being forced to spend the night with him. It's lonely some of the time, but the gratitude in her eyes over breakfast each morning makes him sure that it's worthwhile, that he's doing the right thing.

So he pushes his chair away from the computer and takes her hand, as he usually does when she comes to find him. 'Is there?' he says quietly, although there's nobody else in the house that they might wake. 'Do you want me to get rid of it?'

'You don't believe me, do you?' Another statement, flat and mechanical.

'Of course I do. I just want to know if there's anything I'm supposed to do about it. Should I go and take a look?'

'No.' The quaver in her voice at this takes him quite by surprise, and he stands up. 'It's not safe, Aaron. Don't go down there. I just thought—I thought you should know. About the alligator. Don't go into the kitchen while it's there.'

'Alright, love.' He takes her gently by the arm; she flinches but doesn't protest, lets him lead her over to the sofa and sit her down. 'Do you want to tell me about it?'

'It's big,' she says promptly. 'I've never seen one before; I wasn't expecting it to be so big. And green. And it's got these—eyes, like

237

big blue stones, all hard and cold.' He puts his arm around her; she makes as if to pull away, then seems to change her mind and moves into his embrace, her head on his shoulder.

'It's got blue eyes?' He keeps his voice soft. Her hair tickles his cheek.

'Big blue eyes. Like a child's. Maybe it's a baby alligator.'

'But then how did it get to be so big?'

'I don't know,' she says earnestly. 'I think maybe alligators are a lot bigger than we thought they were. I mean, we've only ever seen pictures of them. Have you ever been to a zoo? Have you ever seen an alligator at the zoo?'

'No.' Not an out-and-out lie; he's been to zoos before, but he doesn't remember ever having seen an alligator at one. He recalls crocodile enclosures, and there's a niggling feeling at the back of his mind that he might have seen one in the flesh once, but there's no point in upsetting her, not when there's an alligator in the middle of the kitchen floor.

'So maybe alligators are bigger than most people think. We wouldn't know. This is our first alligator.'

'I suppose so.' He touches his lips to her forehead and she shuts her eyes, pushes the tip of her nose into the hollow at the base of his throat. Her skin is cold. 'Do you think it's going to hurt us, my love?'

'It's only a baby,' she says quietly. 'It's probably confused. I don't think they can climb stairs, anyway; if we keep quiet and stay up here, I don't think it's going to hurt us. It'll probably be gone by morning.'

'How do you know?'

'That's how it works. That's how everything works.'

'Is it?'

'You don't believe me.' She pulls away from him and sits up. 'You don't think that at all. I know that. I know you. Why won't you argue with me? You always used to argue with me when you thought I was wrong.'

'I don't think you're wrong. And it doesn't matter, does it? I'll stay out of the kitchen until morning, like you asked, if it means you won't worry. So don't worry about it. I don't mind—'

'It's not about whether you mind or not. I'm just trying to

keep you safe. Can't you see that?'

'I know you are.'

'But you don't know! You don't have any proof, and it's—God, Aaron, it's so ridiculous! Can't you see that? Why won't you argue with me?'

'Maybe I don't feel like arguing tonight.' It's the best response he can get out, because no matter how many times he sees her flick from one mood to another in five seconds flat he cannot reconcile himself to it. He worries a moment later that he sounded too sharp, and about a split second after that that he was right.

'It's because you don't believe me.' She licks her lips, looks him solemnly in the eye. 'You don't believe anything I say anymore, do you? It's because I've been like this for so long that you don't trust me. You've stopped having any faith in me at all but you're too scared to say anything in case I get upset. You don't even like me, you don't—'

He hears the accusation implicit in her voice, reaches for her and can't quite bring himself to stop even when she pulls back, holding herself rigidly away from him. 'Come on, love.' There's a pleading in his voice he can't help but despise. 'You know it's nothing like that. I believe you, of course I do, please don't be upset, I . . .'

She comes to him slowly, lowering herself into his arms as if he might attack her, leans her head stiffly on his shoulder and lets him murmur soothingly into her ear, the way he always does, the way she always lets him, eventually. He tells her that he loves her. He tells her that nothing has changed, and that he believes her, the way he always does, even if she can't see it. That he has faith in her. That he is sorry.

It's halfway through this stream of guilt that he realises she's been crying for almost five minutes. He falls silent, strokes her hair; her shoulders pulse briefly, rhythmically against his hold for a moment, and then she falls still.

'You have to promise me you won't go down there,' she whispers, and although the collar of his shirt is wet he can hear no trace of the tears in her voice. 'It'll be gone by morning, but it's dangerous there now. You have to promise me.'

'I won't go down there.' He means it.

She swallows and pushes him away gently, getting unsteadily to her feet. 'I'm going to bed, then. You promise you won't go into the kitchen?'

'I promise.'

'All right.' She walks to the door, lays her hand on the doorframe and pauses, turning back to look at him; the light from the corridor dimly highlights her figure. 'Aaron.'

'Yes?'

'I'm sorry. I didn't mean to say all those things, I . . .'

He pulls himself upright, holds his back straight and smiles at her as reassuringly as he's able. 'Don't be sorry, love.'

The smile she gives him in return makes her look ill. 'I really— I'm really trying, you know.'

'I know.'

'I'll get there someday.'

'I know that too.' He wonders if he should go to her, but she shakes her head as he makes to stand up and he settles obediently back into his seat. 'Get some sleep. It's nearly five.'

She hovers a moment longer and then vanishes, closing the living room door behind her. A moment later he hears the faint 'click' of the landing switch and sees the cracks of light in the doorway vanish. At some length he gets up, moves over to the computer he abandoned almost half an hour ago (was she only there that long?) and switches it off. He takes off his jumper and tosses it carelessly onto the back of the chair. He sits back down and shuts his eyes, feeling his shoulders sag into the sofa cushions, a steady, insistent pounding starting at his temples.

He thinks about his wife of just under a year getting into the bed they no longer share; he imagines her laying her head on his pillow and closing her eyes. In his imagination she smiles a little as she drifts into sleep. He wonders if this is really the case, and if it would really make so very much difference to him if it were.

He thinks about the alligator in the middle of the kitchen floor and its impossible size; in his mind it blinks its cold blue child's eyes at him and swishes its tail. He sees each scale in its vivid, poisonous green, and the black claws digging into the tiled floor. The house creaks and groans soothingly; he hears scraping in the darkness, and recalls vaguely that he's right above their kitchen.

He wonders, dimly, where the alligator came from, and what it is doing here. After all, it must have escaped from somewhere, unless it swam the ocean from Africa and crossed the mainland without being spotted—some distant zoo where all the funding goes on the crocodile enclosure. But why here, in their house? Does it have some higher purpose? Is it there to warn them or protect them, or to frighten them?

It doesn't matter, he tells himself, shifting against the sofa cushions. It's probably confused; it's only a baby, and it'll be gone by morning.

She's trying, you know. Really trying.

You never argue with me anymore.

He falls asleep.

Imani Sims

Biography

Imani Sims is a Seattle native who spun her first performance poem at the age of fourteen. Since then, she has developed an infinitely rippling love for poetry in all of its forms. She believes in the healing power of words and the transformational nuance of the human story. Imani is the founder of Split Six Productions (splitsix.com), an interdisciplinary art production company that works towards connecting artists and collecting POC stories for production on stage. Her book *Twisted Oak* is available on Requiem Press and her second collection *Beloved:Collision* is available via Amazon.

POSTURED

She has decided
To stop bitch
Beg and bend
Knees. She has
Decided to paint
Her nails instead.

She has found
There is more
Uprising in bright
Pink, than there
Will ever be
In bent knee.

So she paints
And smiles deep,
Paints and smiles
Deep.

And What of Oz

She has decided
To see light
Where once she
Saw glittered shoes
And no clicked
Heels to home.

The song that
Led this charge
Has stopped being
The nail in
Left ventricle but
Became the melody
Of push past.

Also, there is
Nothing as encouraging
As it being Friday
And she only
Needs the sheets
And sleep for
Two days. Silent.

XI: STRENGTH

Gather the pieces
She said, lion
By the mouth,

Collect your demons,
Slay them with
Your teeth, spit

Out their bones
In reverse, so
To chew these
Roles forward, again.
They are not

Yours. They belong
To the one
Slain by bedside

Table, bleeding into
Floor vents, staining
Carpet. Collect her

Twelfth rib, keep
It. Remind yourself
Of your sacred.

Never
        Look
                Back.

YEMAYA: BLACK MERMAID

She remembers herself
As scales, translucent

Water slick decoration
Always attached to

Skin, but today
Rainbow flaked shield

Becomes defiant declaration.

Keith Jarrett

Biography

Keith Jarrett writes poetry and short fiction. In 2010, he simultaneously held the titles of London Poetry Slam Champion and UK Poetry Slam Champion. He has since run workshops and co-ordinated school poetry festivals in the UK and beyond.

In 2013, his five-star reviewed poetry show *Identity Mix-Up* debuted at the Edinburgh Fringe festival. In 2014, he completed the pioneering Spoken Word Educators programme, teaching in a secondary school while studying for an MA at Goldsmiths University; he also won the Rio International Poetry Slam championship at the FLUPP favela literary festival.

Keith's fiction has appeared in anthologies and magazines, including *Attitude* and *Tell Tales IV*. His influences range from Caribbean trickster figures to Latin American surrealist authors. He is writing his first novel and a new collection of his poems will be published early next year.

TEN WAYS TO AVOID
HEARING HIM SAY SORRY

I
Change the subject.
The weather is plentiful; the rain is problematic;
the third stair still snitches on you, even years later
when you try to creep upwards unnoticed.

II
This close up, your dad's head
is like the large Dutch pot above
the kitchen cupboard. Leave
that to stew for a few minutes.

III
In Latin American Spanish
'*ahorita*' is an imprecise way of saying 'not quite
now'. Sound it out slowly. Feel your tongue curl
up on the 'r'. Flick it out like a Swiss knife.

IV
No entiendo inglés.

V
Use find and replace to destroy the word
or press backspace till your PC beeps a void.

VI
Beat him to it.
I'm sorry I didn't answer your texts.
I'm sorry for ever being fifteen years old.
I'm sorry I took the knife out the house. It wasn't like that. I promise.

VII
Sorry isn't the hardest word to say;
for me, it's 'world' and the way it whirls empty
in my mouth.

If you're Yonosuke,
the Japanese student I taught,
'scrawl' will sound like a mess
of consonants surrounding one lonely vowel.
It is one of many things you cannot vocalise.

VIII
The search engine told me
in Japanese, I'm sorry
is pronounced: *Suminasen.*

IX
Lo siento.

X
I am sitting on the third stair of our conversation
in a home I lost the keys to, many years ago,
sifting through letters that still come in my name
and I want to look you in the eyes and tell you
it's ok.

ON MY CASE (AFTER A BREAK-UP)

First, the instrumentals: hi-hats, dirty bass,
and a theme I lean back to on a gloomy Sunday.

Then, the book I'll never read again: my mind too stacked
to reach for the shelf, my spine too slack to give it away:

there are endings and there are endings.

I have a big heart on one of the two Valentines cards I left
unsent. The cellophane wrap reads: *blank on the inside*.

I'll leave them be, like the unspent Euros lining the pen pot
with other foreign objects: hollow pen lids; broken buttons.

I'll leave them

like my headphones, hanging
on the end of a nod, plugged into nothing

but this Sunday and the shadows
and the phone that rings and rings

and knows I won't pick up.

Playing His Music on Shuffle (Or how friend 'A' describes the random encounter)

. . .And then the inevitable happened: an unfortunately-timed
leaking of Clark Sister divas, Kim Burrell riffs and full-blown
hallelujah chorus choirs he didn't even know he possessed
gospel-slapped the 2am night when he plugged in his phone.

And he still refers to it as the accident: he fled the man's home,
fearful of a God who punishes men who lay with men, blown
away by sinful desires, with eternal fire and Mary Mary. And now
he builds playlists, lays down tracks before getting laid on Grindr.

I think that probably makes him a considered lover
but I wonder if the real accident isn't in his playlist
but in the playground where he downplays the full
range of his repertoire. His bed rocks to predictable.

I hope he encounters love with a man he can dance with
on random shuffle, with the lights on, right to the end
of his songlist; who embraces all of his hidden tracks.

Because then, there'll be hope for us all.

III

This is a post-Marxist/ post-feminist/ postcolonialist/ post-gender
queer/ post racism/ post postmodernist/ post post-retro/ post
hetero/ post-poetry poem

this poem is too cute to take on terms like intersectionality
or misogyny
or reality

this poem is drowning in the floods
created by the UK Independence Party
and gay marriage
and the two men in the Macklemore music video holding hands
and jumping
into a sea of convention

this poem is intentionally stuck somewhere in 2013
wearing YOLO and Geek t-shirts
licking rusty hammers and swinging on dirty machinery
it is twerking on the head of a blurred line
it is being lawfully shot at by police in Tottenham at the same time
history is being revised

the camera doesn't lie
and neither does this poem
but the truth hurts like a badly-timed cliché
and your ears are closed

check your fucking privilege   says this poem
question authority   says this poem
resist the government, take your stroke-
prone finger away from your chin
and use it to drum
on the skin of rebellion   says this poem

the water is troubled
this poem is unsettled
its lines are drawn.

MIDNIGHT DRINKS:
I AM NOT DECEIVED . . .

after Gwendolyn Brooks

The air of your kiss is so close I can nearly taste the inside. I
am the dead silence within clasped hands; held breath. I am
a squatter in the fickle city of your possibilities. But I will not
shelter in your simple grin tonight, another of your deceived
lovers leaving a skeleton halo in your closet. In my clumsy, I
push this pregnant pause between our words away, make do
with bad impressions, clown away the inevitable. So. . . it's not
a good idea, I will say. Then, maybe tomorrow. Then, I think
I will go home now. And if I read the low of the pint glass, it
will tell me I am drowning. The meniscus clings, it slides, is
losing the uphill struggle. After you order another, I am still
holding my breath, and my tongue, and your smile is summer
at the height of your seasoned gestures. I hold them. Because
I know too well the climax of this manufactured meet. At the
end of the emoticon in your texts is lonely. At the end, as sun
burns new, we will see all this in a new light. Your kiss stays
under our breath, waiting to emerge, and I lean forward and
reach for the glass. I swig, swipe at an imagined fly. The birds
on my phone catapult away in anger. The butterflies continue
to flick at my bowels. Neither of us shifts. Nothing is going to
happen, I think, just before you lean right in and my lips sing.

THE DISAPPOINTMENT

By the time I descend the stairs again and open the kitchen door, there are cupboards flying open everywhere. Mum pulls packets down on tiptoes, stretching her doughy arms out. It's a habit of years; she does this practically without looking now. Among the chaos of the cupboards, stacked high with out-of-date herbs and spices, is an order only she can smell and feel. Each labelled jar has a slightly distinct shape—depending on the brand—placed in varying positions so she can get at them without climbing the step ladder to look.

She pours powder into the bowl, replaces a packet, opens the next cupboard, retrieves a jar and pinches some differently-coloured granules over the other pile. Her head disappears and reappears like some magic trick behind the wooden doors.

I marvel for a while at how involved she seems, so completely unaware of my entrance, until, after stirring the ingredients with the silver spoon, she swivels her head towards me and speaks.

'See if you can reach up into the cupboard there and fetch me the cinnamon. I can't find the new packet.'

I place my container down on the counter and sigh long and deep. I squeeze past her, ignoring the plump of her rump and the tightness of the kitchen.

'You could have closed the door back!' she huffs, shuffling over to the door and closing us in again, until the steam once more clouds out the world beyond the panes and the yeast smell invades my senses.

If I'd been a better man, I would have been able to buy her a kitchen as large as the house. And I would have filled it with children who giggle and laugh with their grandmother, baking cookies and making cakes. There would be space to run and have flour fights. And mum would half-heartedly scold them for eating too much cake mixture.

I crane my head back to scan the top shelf of the cupboard and instantly spot the packet of cinnamon powder. I reach up and pull it down.

'No, not the powder I want. I add some of that already. It's the sticks I want, to give him some sweetness.'

'You've already added cinnamon?'

'Yes, for the colouring and thing. Now I want some more to give some flavour. Don't you worry—I know what I'm doing!'

'Ok, mum, I was just saying—'

'Well, don't just say!'

I fumble around on tiptoes for a while before I find the sticks of cinnamon. I can't help bringing it to my nose until mum taps my hand and I give them to her.

'We don't have much time left. You bring your essence?'

I feel my face go hot. 'Yes, mum.'

The container I brought down is behind me. I suppose I should feel more embarrassed. My essence she called it. Barely two tablespoons worth of liquid, and it looks unhealthy, to say the least. When she looks at it, she'll probably be able to tell I smoke heavily, that I drink too much and eat too little. My diet consists of caffeine, nicotine, ibuprofen and whisky. Cocaine and Viagra on a good week (and good weeks are so increasingly rare these days). Haagen Dazs on a bad one. Cereal bars and chewing gum if it's mediocre. My essence is viscous alright, but it has the colour of too many nights misspent, and too many days living like a poet. A wanderer.

'Okay, just hold onto it a sec.' Mum lifts the Dutch pot lid. Something is boiling inside. She sniffs, makes an approving nod and then turns down the gas.

I envy my mother's prowess in the kitchen. The confident way in which she stirs and peels, dips fingers into boiling liquids and measures ingredients with her mind. I've always been a stickler for the recipe book. Precise teaspoon measurements. Jugs of all sizes down to the last millilitre.

I tried cooking ackee and saltfish once, for a lover (I did have a lover, once). I phoned mum three times, asking her what ratio of ackee to saltfish the first time—ratio, what you mean, ratio?—and then, the second time around, I asked how many minutes before I added the ackee to the peppers and onions. Finally, I phoned and asked her how much of the tinned tomato I should add. I could hear her face explode over the phone, just before she hung up. In the end, we ate at a MacDonald's; a happy meal, if there ever was one.

'OK, son, hand it to me.'

I pass her the container and notice my hands are shaking. I put them straight in my pockets. Mum creases her nose at the liquid and then spoons half of it into the pot on the fire. It makes an unpleasant spitting sound then stops.

'You're not putting all of it in?'

'You mad? Look at it! I'm not having Sammy turn out nothing like you!'

'Sammy—?'

'If I did have a choice I would have used something else, or someone else, but this will have to do.' She points to the container and the gooey mixture and I can't disagree. I wouldn't want that to contaminate the recipe, either. I look away, stand back. If there are onions in that pot, they must be stinging my eyes. I don't wipe them though. My hands are staying in my pockets.

I'm craving a cigarette now, so I try to talk and distract myself. I'm also starting to feel the drain; my speech is slurring.

'You're naming him Sammy?'

'Yes. Don't speak his name!' she snaps. 'Please,' she whispers afterwards, as the contents of the pot bubble erratically.

I once heard that when you call out someone's name, it ties them to the Earth. Just repeating the name, Sammy, fills me with the realisation that this concoction in a bowl is soon to become alive; it has also made me feel dizzy and otherworldly. Soon I am to be discarded and replaced.

'Why did you choose that name?'

'Why you worry your head with so much rubbish, eeh—?'

'I was just asking—!'

'Everything you say, you was just asking, you was just saying, you was just doing. Why you can't just shut up and not bother me, yah? You can't see I'm trying to do something worthwhile with what's left of you?'

I've seen her make that face before, in the brief seconds between discovering some rancid, forgotten ingredient in the depths of the fridge and disposing of it. I purse my lips. I do more than purse; I bite. I feel the trickle of blood and suck on it. It tastes of metal and salt.

I stay quiet and watch the pattern of steam on the glass. Mum takes the hand off her hip and resumes her cooking, all the while humming a tune. I try to place it—a lullaby perhaps? Her cooking song, which she used to sing while we were children? It is so familiar, yet out of my grasp. I open my mouth to ask her but remember just in time to keep my mouth shut.

Mum closes a cupboard or two above her head. The contents of the pot bubble again. She blurs out of focus for a while. My head throbs and I feel nauseous. I think she senses this and returns to the bowl where the dough and the spice mix are. Using gloves to pick up the grey pot, she pours in a little of the liquid, stirs, adds more; stirs, adds more; stirs.

Everything is whirring in my head and I would like to sit down, I think. In another life, I would have bought her a large kitchen, as big as this house. There would be a counter with stools; tall, leather-cushioned stools you get in these modern houses. There would be smart wooden floorboards and none of this cheap lino. Gleaming tiles with no cracks.

Sammy won't be a disappointment like I am. He will be handsome and smart, agile and wise. He will deliver a litter of children and a sackful of gold with every paycheque. There will be houses and SUVs and holidays abroad and spa retreats.

His odour is the odour of sweet success. Cinammon and honey fill my nostrils. Cayenne powder and whole scotch bonnet peppers are his constitution. His belly is fire. He is not a coward like me. He is a go-getter. Someone not to be messed with. Someone who will make his mother proud.

Somewhere through the mist in my eyes, I can see my mother shake her hips as she continues humming. Her sway is youthful. Yes, Sammy will make her proud.

I feel so faint; I know there is little left of me. My mother pours the ingredients back into the Dutch pot and my eyes seal closed. It's now time to put everything in the oven.

BARNABY CALLABY

BIOGRAPHY

Barnaby Callaby is a collagist concerned with how poetry might manipulate an image. He edits his work the way a designer or film-maker might: conscious of the transformations amidst image and art. Partial to collaboration, Barnaby is inspired by a mutating poetry—shaped and reshaped at the impulse of other minds. Coursing madly toward an immersive and intentionally modern form, there's unrest in his work: the churn of travel sickness, a side effect of being launched in two directions at once.

COVER

We talked the thin out of the air last night
Now we're clinging
Under high tog duvet
Short of breath
Your eyes were on your head last night
Like a wig
Yes I felt the clips
I didn't mind
But nearly asked why you stopped my hands from blowing your
cover

EYE TEST

Start again,
Ask the student nurse:
Can I answer your questions,
follow up this appointment?
I want to be a patient again—as soon as possible.
He smiles,
because I'm trouble.
In the dark I ask him,
Which is clearer:
1 or 2?

TAUNTING LOVE

Forgiveness is not like love,
It is shaped like crime and people.
Love is the brick surrounded by glass,
Taunted perhaps:
By calls we didn't answer.

An object appears to shape us,
Concrete as blood and buildings.
An airport in the village
Uproots us from home.
An object in a person,
A person in an object.

LONG ISLAND ICE TEA

The bar turns lids,
unwired dials and bottles of lemonade
into ice and coke,
like I wouldn't at home:
Long Island Ice Tea.
The band have beers but want to unscrew water.
Music fans wave full glasses,
go in for froth like making clumsy scoops at popcorn.
At the Jazz event,
hot table.
Men here together,
sliding candle holders,
cycling home on a full stomach.

MARILYN AT THE SALFORD LOWRY

'O, Time
Be Kind...'
'...Ease my mind,
While you eat my flesh.'
—Marilyn Monroe

It's spring outside and Marilyn's driven to distraction.
A woman in a raincoat stares,
makes the suggested donation.
She dreams she is lifted out,
run away with, far from gallery walls.

The woman in a raincoat's straining,
searching for herself in the glass.
Squinting at Marilyn
like she's some dirty mirror.
Beyond the coloured mask she lingers,
Venus of Hollywood.
It's spring outside
and she can feel her stiletto heel piercing the moor.

The yellow perm, the hourglass cheeks,
pink eyelids pop! unfeeling.
But there: hands deep in raincoat pockets,
a woman shares
in dreaming.

PORTER

I woke up last night worried
That I'd forgotten the lemonade for table 31.
One day it suddenly rained and people changed places.
I came inside and heard the waiters shout,
31 are now on 45,
24 has become 47,
26 is 49.

It's raining.
People are walking away without paying.
Where's the lemonade for table 31?
31 is 45.
Then someone rings for room service.
And I'm glad.

The kitchen is underground.
The restaurant is all fussy. I'm feeling down.
Room service!
I can look in the mirror
As I ride the steady elevator
That's tinted gold and flattering.
It makes me look well.

I work here,
Honestly.
What do you think I'm doing, selling buttons?
(If you want one see me after the show.)
No, I'm Porter: a waiter, dogsbody.
Helping people that already have the upper hand.
Providing excellent service.
Knowing what people want before they want it.
Answering doors before they're knocked,
Phones before they ring.

I'm encouraged to read minds;
Encouraged to pay every little task mind,
So I can do them in my sleep.
So I do do them in my sleep
And wake up in the middle of the night worried
That I'd forgotten the lemonade for table 31
That are now on 45.

Sometimes I have to ask myself if I'm hearing voices
Or am I really reading minds?

I think of nice hotels
Where maids seem made-up
And drop behind the walls in secret lifts
Like shielded nosebleeds.

Here special guests try hotel sex,
Have double honeymoons,
And feel the hips of pushed together beds.
Where people second sleep after buffets,
Cringe as housekeeping knocks.

Rooms and rooms.
I think of rent and all that space:
The games room,
The spotlight stage.
How they offset the empty beds with constant one-off events.

I think of rent,
Debt,
The special guests
That ask for room service
And one off events.

Knock.
The guest has the upper hand.
I announce myself; I knock.

Explain myself—*room service.*
They get to open the door,
Reveal themselves at whatever speed they like.

My hands are full.
I'm carrying something hot and often heavy for them to eat,
And then I see him.
He's wearing nothing under the dressing gown;
The lights aren't all the way up.
He wants to feel at home.
For me to bring silver service down the corridor
Right to the foot of his bed.

And he thinks,
Like the tables that became 47 and 45,
My values can suddenly change too.
But, like an angel,
I say yes without thinking
And review my scruples
Invisibly.

I give good service as a table
On hands and knees,
Let him eat from the small of my back.

I grit my teeth
As he pushes his food around.
He tips me.
Makes me feel the weight of the upper hand.

BURN

SCENE 1. (CAROL)

An easel turned away from the audience.

SFX: Rain sound starts and continues for full duration.

CAROL AND KIDS:

The kids were excited to swim through their flooded home,
Working in London didn't wash.
Float,
Once a head.
The ball of wood,
Shaped by drowning,
Bobbing out of the stove's reach.
Passing through the telly room proved hard for them too,
And I splashed in the brown water.
We'll go to a restaurant tonight,
Get something to eat.

Polished by traction, had the stuffing knocked out of it,
We had fished from the reeds
Wood like white meat.
What had we restored by the fire:
A carved pear, doll part, a missing boule?
Vincent wanted it in the pile,
The slats on the hearth.

As the ash wood whirled,
Rotating to stationary music.
I was with my children,
Resenting how dry it had been.

SCENE 2. (ADRIAN)

*Adrian slowly starts to sit in mid air. A chair is brought centre stage so
Adrian can land in the chair.*

*A plant pot with black pole stuck in it is brought on right in front of the
chair.*

Easel rotated to reveal Ladder of Fire image.

*Adtian stands, produces apple from pocket and sticks it on end of pole.
Sits with apple obstructing face.*

TIN-CAN:

The Kids were excited to call thcir kitten 'Tin Can'
It was a joke I didn't understand
But it didn't make me angry
I'd call him Tom Cat behind his back

I got in at midnight
The man of the house to find the family ganging round him
Shouting answers over a phone-in
The ends of evening TV
Why is everyone downstairs?
The eye drops from the medicine drawer?
Raw shaven skin on the back of Tin-Can's neck?
We had to take him to the vet.
I was worried again
Like when Carol told me my son was shaving now.
And the vet gave you those?
No—these are left over from the dog.
The Kid's blind dog that ran away—Belka
another name I wouldn't say
Dog in Russian
Bella I called her
until everyone dropped the 'K'

Slides apple up as if it's floating in a flood, stands and finishes poem with it at face level again when standing.

Because of Tin-Can we stopped finding wood on Sunday
But I'd search the house to keep the fire burning

It was winter and the cards were arriving
rows of tooth ache amounting on my desk
I used to light the fire to remind the kids I still made it home
Let them smell the smoke in the morning
smoke I shared a whiskey with
In four hours I'd be back
to Christmas cards without their names on
The ones that made me think of counterparts
cards submitted to Carol and Kids

Scene 3. (Carol)

Lights fail and in darkness the performer's hat is swapped for a lightbulb hat.

Carol climbs to stand on the chair and switches the bulb on.

Shivering and wet/cold.

Carol:

I was excited at the flood warning
at the presence of water and everything
I left the house to be alone
in the arrowhead of runoff and sideways rain
I felt myself turning downslope
to a voluptuous river
now swollen like made up lips
I noticed swans aside the current
finding moments of calm to guide their young
over layers of water
curvaceous lightning
biting at the river's planetary cheeks
I took my children there as if to paddle
but to see what had risen with the table

The kids were excited to swim through their flooded home
Working in London didn't wash
Float
Once a head
The ball of wood
Shaped by drowning.

Taking the deliberate strides
required by mud
We took the wood like white meat

Pushing legs through the telly room was hard for them too
And I splashed in the brown water
We'll go to a restaurant tonight
Get something to eat

We restored by the fire
A carved pear, doll part, garden boule
Until Vincent set it down in the pile
the slats on the hearth

The flood came through our door like Christmas cards,
uplifting, out of the stove's reach.

As the ash wood whirled,
rotating to stationary music.
I was with my children,
resenting how dry it had been.

Turns lightbulb off.

END

BRYONY BATES

BIOGRAPHY

Bryony Bates is the winner of the Allan Horsfall Prize in the Young Enigma Awards. The Allan Horsfall Prize celebrates LGBT young writers in Greater Manchester, and is sponsored by Archives+ at Manchester Central Library. Bryony is currently Archives+ Writer in Residence, where she is exploring the LGBT collections.

THE ART OF DYING

Suffer eyes more drawn down from the operation
and burst her that thick cloud was god.
I was answered in the sweet hair clinging, and black, all throughout the bone.
This is a Revelation that Jesus Christ
made in Sixteen Shewings, or Revelations particular.
Four at the hospital, and bloodless with dignity
during the th- to the Father.
She from my body has long suffered thus I would help
In this deep dying.
Little waxen above a child
I just started to smash the dishes.
I came in here and I broke my heart.
You just learn to cope a bit better.

I have yet to die, I have yet the thorns
were left, all left, all changed of his will
but all of the hospital came where—mourning,
Families of clicking bodies plenteously bleeding
drawn out of Christ, grief to the child,
Thinking of grief, pale dying, more pleasing
loneliness—that sometimes I saw
in the fiend overcome, overcome as
we bide in the sweetness of nails.

Blessed and angry for I would be purged
by the mercy of God and the thought of her hands
under the doctors to distance myself,
to lead eyes to hold her, nightmares to think of her.

Bodies are broken full deep into tender flesh
piercing and dried, to smash the small hands
and I never thought that I'd have—I had to
be the sort of person to—I trust you
It's going to, yes, hurt to do it together,
but when the time comes, I'd understand, yes.

Allan Horsfall's Homosexual Problem

'Have you a homosexual problem? Ring Bolton 62783 or Manchester 8325253.'

When exploring the LGBT artefacts at Archives+, I saw the words above at least ten times. They were neatly typewritten with a courteous message to whom it may concern, asking that this ad be placed in the classified section of a local paper. I also saw several letters of refusal, and at least one attempt to charge more than the going rate for the ad to be placed.

It is strange what you can learn about someone from the scraps they leave behind. These letters, written in the 1960s, are from the papers of Allan Horsfall, late Manchester gay activist, found in Archives+.

I learned, I think, that Mr Horsfall was humane, determined, and firmly believed in making a reasonable request. When he was not met with a reasonable response—the *Manchester Evening News* refusing to carry his advert, for example, while running lurid stories of homosexual blackmail—it seems he was bemused, and perhaps a little annoyed, and he wrote another letter.

I don't mean he was dispassionate. He devoted his life to a cause he believed in—what more can be said? And among apologies for absences because of flu, and reimbursements for the train to Hull, a letter starting, 'I seem to remember that you told me, somewhere, sometime—through a wonderful alcoholic haze...'

His sense of humour, too, speculating about the motives of a judge who sent a 17-year old boy to Borstal for a minor offence with the hope of curbing his homosexuality: 'Just what, I wonder, did that man, and those who thought like him, imagine went on in our Borstals.'

I found Allan's papers fun, with their quaint phrases and rows of typed x's to blot out mistakes. But in the aftermath of Manchester Pride—a time when we typically parade through the streets of Manchester together, here, and queer, and glittery, and pissed—I read over and over letters to Allan from all kinds of people—from social workers and friends and maybe some of the people who had seen those adverts in the local paper.

Being gay used to be very lonely. It still is, still can be for many people all over the world and right here. Though it is so much easier for us to find each other. The first time I heard someone who grew up in the 1950s say that they had thought they were literally the only person in the world who felt this way, I was shocked. How couldn't you know? But then, how could you know when there was no one like you, anywhere in sight? Not in your town, not in films or on television—nowhere.

Allan knew that this was wrong. There are gay people everywhere and he knew that as well as a change in the law—endless letters to MPs about the Sexual Offences Act—gay people needed to know each other. To know, beyond something furtive in the street, that there is someone like you. So he wrote on behalf of his North Western Homosexual Law Reform Committee to place those ads in the classified section.

From a letter which I think was signed 'Harry' from 10 February 1968: 'I hope the work your committee is doing will progress and be appreciated for it is something which is a constantly recurring event for some unfortunate boy or girl. That's why I feel that this work is so important.'

And from John Holland, 19-years old in 1968: 'I now have all I want—a husband and a future.'

The work Allan Horsfall did is so important.

A lot of my writing is based on taking what other people have written or said—especially casual, everyday encounters—and turning it into my own, so having access to such a large collection of material is fantastic.

I entered the Young Enigma Awards after attending a writing workshop at the library which used materials from the archives. I hope I can get other people similarly inspired—it worked for me.

Janette Ayachi

Biography

Janette Ayachi is the winner of Young Enigma's Barbara Burford Prize for LGBT writers aged 18-35 across the UK, supported by Commonword. Janette has appeared in anthologies such as *New Writing Scotland, Journeys through Fire*, and the *Up Do Anthology of Women's Fiction*. She has been shortlisted for a number of awards, including the StAnza Digital Slam, Lancelot Andrewes Award 2012 and Write Queer London 2012. She won the Museum of St Andrews/StAnza Competition with her poem 'Pucara Bull'. Her pamphlets are *Pauses at Zebra Crossings* (Original Plus Press, 2012) and *A Choir of Ghosts* (Calderwood Press, 2013).

GRAVITY

(For P.C)

'Every comet throws an arc
And scars our vision 'cross the dark'
(Shirley Manson, *Beloved Freak*)

When two comets collide to stain
 the white sheets of the Stratosphere Hotel
 where tequila talks, cocktails listen,
cheap champagne blurs even bionic vision
 machine-dark of the dance floor fixes our gaze
 on artificial smoke swallowing outlines of its prey
like staring at a constellation from the trenches
this place for queer Utopia to rise from the ashes:
 fags, dykes, trannies, cross dressers, clowns,
 lost snow queens in stilettos, sulphur-crowned
with energy and bar mirrors where lips stick
 behind curtains of the Baronial towers of toilets
 where all the beloved freaks of society circuit colour
into disjointed rainbows, shooting arcs of neon
and the love that dare not speak its name is screaming
 and everyone is dancing or talking about dancing
 like spirits self-rooted under the arm pits of trees
gossip stirs a timber boom across a frieze of speakers
 couples at tables warm their hands on the undertow.

Digits on screen before the dial and waving holographic smiles
  echo where this is supposed to be a love poem
  the undeniable crush and kismet of connection
when parallel with my virtual doll for the first time
  her long hair like a serpentine midnight river
  tracing its glorious way over my face and down
to where butterflies transformed into a cage of stars
  her laugh so potently desirable I trapped it in a bottle
  with solar-strength ion tails of ice and dust
close enough to the sun now to be nucleus with our lust
  all urgent pulse and streaming jets in our wake
  from the internet ether to real-time orbit
we carry our mystery, our weight, depend on the magnitude
  of gravity to pull us closer in or further away.

Hedonism with an Ice-Cream Shot

White bed beneath a bay window
a perfect geometry of twigs and stars
my tongues pharmaceutical tendencies
hooked on your skin
bird song stills the square
outside Kensington Court Hotel
sodden leaves pile into corners like sand
a distant drill cracks its fist against tarmac.

Polish maids gossip through walls
as I rearrange the score of echoes
from the ceremony at Southwark Cathedral
its tangle of spires, a cold crematorium,
a daft spectre but still I lit a candle
at the base of the only entrance into London
across the druid river for centuries;
princes, paupers, prelates, prostitutes, poets,
playwrights, prisoners, and patients
all found refuge here- I have played my part in each.

I dress my wardrobe in black
more shades possible than Van Dyke
and I expire in strangers beds.

Two nights of hedonism in Soho
the Singaporean squatter poet
who was pinned by a weight I could not shift
and the Spanish dancer who tugged at every
string of my puppet-heart
one night sleeping in her hair, softness beyond silk,
her three final words as we unbound ourselves
in the street, the last lingering finger-tip release
the air filling with our energy, stripped bare for flight
– it was an ending even the sky couldn't fit.

Faun

The boys from Inverleith schools
seem more interested in each other
than the chewing gum-smiles of girls,
old men kick up leaves in these streets
dreaming of the goat-smell of locker rooms.

LOVE TRIANGLE: PART ONE

You would come back tired from your martial arts class
let me pin you down, my weight above you pressing
your pelvic bone with my open thighs, your wrists
with my palms. And we would kiss for hours
until the room darkened and our mouths
pulsed with a current of terrific stars
our hair ruffled into thick ringlets
where we kept our secrets
you never let me unlock your gate
your garden bloomed and I trimmed
fingers over holy lands, southern crosses
a ravine of pounding wolves, hothouse orchids
like an astrologer tracking isolation and meteorites
through a slide-door of many mirrors how you gasped
to bite me as my tongue tampered with words and elastic

only to later knock the keys from music, tease out glissando
suspend me on the landscape of your sculpted body always wanting more.

MERCHANT CITY

I like it here—the radiator and music booms, the waitress wears
trouser-braces and did the most alluring pout as she shook my
margarita cocktail. The two girls on the sofa in front of me hold
hands and talk about the song—I watch their fingers closely, start to
feel lonely, sip faster.

Already I know who is the loved and the lover. One dances at the
bar with her bottle of Budweiser trying to impress, acting like she
knows she is being watched. The other locks into her phone. Red
strobe-glow spills from behind the sofa, the bar is almost on fire
with plastic stars, each table has a candle and everywhere else is
shadow.

Men dressed as women enter the bar, extravagantly in heels and
long-sleeved gloves; they sling shots in profile into false eyelashes
and glitter. The big windows encircle us, the blue lights seeps
in from the outside, alien yet familiar- the stars now in puddles.
The place is flooded with fairy-lights and couples, a distracting
combination—I wait for you even though I know you won't be
coming.

LOVE AND MANY NOTEBOOKS

In the apocryphal illicit side streets of Leith
tenements slacken into cardinal squalor

everyone has eyes like stones
and no one opens their windows.

But this is where you drink, unravel
and I have been watching you

as voyeuristic as a cloud always in the background
of strobe-lit designated smoking areas

where genies spin from lamps
laughing at the current fare for freedom.

All froth and fizz like a spilt glass of champagne
anecdotes bubble to the surface, strike applause

from the shadow-crowd jagged at the edges
like centre aligned text until you buckle them into circle

like the black-plumed horses or hearses in my dreams
who stampede beaming like an astrological clock

the audience sharpening its blades against the night
if only I were made of steel, then I could move closer.

Instead I am vine-twisted over the length of you-
an unsent message, a pencilled invention smudged over time

even on the worlds flipside there is no landscape
with roads which I can unscramble, no glitch in the sky

I can penetrate to stand and gloat at where the future breaks in
like a shamrock separating on Guinness foam, a three piece suit

dismantled in transit, all palpitations instigated across
the body's meridian, sadness rises, a thousand dripping taps

tears on the retina swell the world to blur
the temporal mirage of love all the more beautiful for its momentary fleet

they all came as ritualistic as prayer
the asylum years braiding hair, the vinyl sunsets, and winters last bluebell.

On Keeping a Wolf

(For K.N.M)

Like all the therianthropic women that have tapped
Virgil's sorcerer for his poisonous herbs

I keep the wolf chlorinated with friendship
instead of suffocating her with the trappings of love.

The night we met she appeared straight from the page
of a Gaskell gothic tale with metronome footsteps

fire-proof in lace and velvet
engulfing me like a hurricane on its hind legs.

We leaned into each other over a bar-crowd
of people punctuated like rain

our similarities and superstitions centre aligned
we spoke in furious tangential tongues.

Giddy on her smell of clementine peel, argan and tinder
I rested my head back against the chair where I watched

her corset-tight chest rise and fall as she breathed
until brazen-clad in confessional ink we escaped

to smoke cigarettes and kiss
a feral pawing of retractable flames in doorways.

She invited me to her daylight guise
an antique bookshop in the Grass Market

a fitting cove for a wolf where I clasped her book
like a talisman bullet-proof in its hot-print shield

and imagined what the throat of the heart
would sound like after midnight's sober bell.

We played shop, tourists ask for Kipling and whiskey guides
she tells me where her true love is tied:

to a married man she has known an epoch
she grinned a charge of stockings and lost boys

her pupils' plutonian-dark, as black as my mornings
those last thirty days where grey haired women walked dogs

picked dandelions, tossed sticks along the river of Lethe:
but here, now, she is the white latex of broken stems

an old world language in concertina with the sky
she is African arrow poison dismantling my pulse
and I am running out of places to hide.

Olivia Smith

Biography

Olivia Smith is a 21-year old writer from East London, working in the city. She has been writing poetry sporadically since she was sixteen, because she liked crafting her thoughts so they would make sense to someone else. Olivia spends most of her time listening to folksy, woodsy music and loud, trashy pop music; and reading as much as she can about how writers learned to write.

16

He'll stroke the seam of your jeans
Up and down, slow and soft
And you feel like you're in a movie
      Like every touch is planned,
            Everything around you is electric.
You could grab his hand,
Push your lips to his and
He would kiss you like he knew your name,
Tilt his head just so,
Wind his hand through yours or you could
Cut off the bastard's head,
Throw it in the river,
Watch it swallow him whole—
Let's see how those lips move
Cold and blue.

Kiss the girl you want to kiss,
And fuck her like your parents aren't home.
Those jeans were too small anyway.

Adam Lowe

Biography

Adam Lowe is a writer, publisher and creative producer from Leeds. He currently lives in Manchester, where he is Co-Director of Young Enigma. Adam also runs Dog Horn Publishing and *Vada Magazine*. He is LGBT History Month Poet Laureate and was a finalist in the Transgender category of the 2010 Lambda Literary Awards.

Friend Roulette

Two figures sat in darkness. Laptops open. The darkness between them, a worldwide web.

Mod: Welcome to FriendRoulette. Log in or register?
A: Log in.
Mod: Would you like FriendRoulette to remember these log in details?
A: Yes.
Mod: You are home. You have ONE new message. You have had 23 profile hits this week.
A: Messages.
B: Hey, what's your pleasure?
A: My pleasure?
B: What you looking for? What's your poison, dude?
A: Looking for chat, fun, mates. Etc.
B: Okay.
A: You?
B: Etc.

Blackout.

Mod: Welcome back to FriendRoulette. Log in or register?
A: Log in.
Mod: Log in details remembered. You are home.
A: One new message.
B: Are you there?
A: Yeah. Just got in.
B: Me too.
A: How was your day?
B: Tiring.
A: Yeah?
B: Been shopping with my sister. You?
A: Been at uni.
B: What are you studying?
A: Sociology.
B: Smart.
A: Not really LOL.
B: Well we can pretend ;)

Blackout.

Mod: Welcome back to FriendRoulette. Log in or register?
A: Log in.
Mod: Log in details remembered. You are home.
A: Where are we?
B: We're at the cathedral. Sunlight spools from above.
A: Tell me.
B: I'm telling you. You're on the grass. Skinny jeans. I'm sitting opposite you, licking a rolly sealed.
A: I can taste the glue on your tongue. Can feel your lips kiss the silky skin closed.
B: You're good at this.
A: I suddenly feel creative.
B: Why?
A: I don't know.
B: Come here.
A: Where are you?

Blackout.

Mod: Welcome back to FriendRoulette. You are home.
B: I'm here. Your lips are on me.
A: My tongue slides into your mouth.
B: Your body softens against me even as you harden.
A: I'm so hard.
B: Like a bulb against my leg.
A: Pressing tight against you.
B: I want to fold into you.
A: Unfold me.
B: Light me up.

Blackout.

B: I unfold you. I speak into the blank, open book of you. Breathe words across your pages. You are starting to take shape: listing lines of black. Forming a story. I reach out. I poke you.

B: This is my space. Take a look at me.

B: Come inside, I say. Come inside me.

Blackout.

295

Mod: Welcome back to FriendRoulette. Log in or register?
A: Log in.
Mod: Log in details remembered. You are home.

A: A home I can feel through
in the dark, moving between walls
unnoticed, master of its geometries
as they slumber, unmapped, undrawn.

Mod: Welcome back to FriendRoulette. Log in or register?
B: Log in.
Mod: Log in details remembered. You are home.

B: A home I can fill, a warm
pool of myself, contained
shapely, ready to flow under
doorways, along skirting.

Mod: Welcome back to FriendRoulette. Log in or register?
A: Log in.
Mod: Log in details remembered. You are home.

A: A home I can dream around
me: a welcome artistry, shaped
to the contours of my soft
mathematics, centred, encircled, whole.

Blackout.

Mod: Welcome back to FriendRoulette. Log in or register?
A: Log in.
Mod: Log in details remembered. You are home.
B: We are alone here. This is a world we have created. The
forest at our back is a velvet emerald burst open. The azaleas are
crimson-pink, open chalices brimming with ambrosia. You pick
one from its slim stalk, raise the cup to your mouth, and drink
of the champagne nectar.

A: In the garden you burrow into my soil, and plant yourself in
the bed of me.

Blackout.

Mod: Welcome back to FriendRoulette. Log in or register?
B: Log in.
Mod: Log in details remembered. You are home.
A: What if we met?
B: What?
A: What if it went wrong?
B: It might. That's half the fun.
A: It might go very wrong.
B: It might.

Blackout.

B: You wait by the frozen turkeys,
covered in goosebumps. Through your
joggers I can see your icicle dick,
the shape of it. Long. I've got
my hand on frozen peas, an excuse
to be here at 3am. Just the noise
of shelf-stackers in the crisps aisle,
enough to cover the rustle as you slide
your hand down, revealing a bulge
in white Ginch Gonch. You pop it
out, creamy as a Mini Milk, and stroke
it gently, working forefinger and thumb
towards the tip. I don't move
but I watch, as you spill spunk
all over the cryo-sleep poultry.

B: I buy the peas, some milk,
and a Calippo, and checking
my palm, I feel short-changed.

Blackout.

A: I need to go.
B: What?
A: I need to get out.
B: Why?
A: I've been sat in this darkness for days with you. I'm spinning
in darkness.
B: What?
A: I need to see what's outside.
B: You know what's outside. It's the same as it's always been. It's

297

only in here that things can change.

A: I'm stuck in FriendRoulette waiting for the loaded chamber.

B: Pardon?

A: The bullet in the gun.

B: Yes, the bullet's in the gun.

A: No. I need to see what's out there. To see if it really exists any more.

B: But isn't this perfect here?

A: It is but . . .

B: What?

A: It's not real.

B: It's real enough. Virtually.

A: I'm not so sure.

B: It was enough for you before.

A: Yes.

B: Will the outside be enough?

A: I'm not sure. Maybe I need both?

B: So you'll come back?

A: Maybe.

B: Maybe?

A: Tomorrow, we might both be somebody new.

Blackout.

A: This is the way out. I can see it up ahead. Bright.
Sunlight. People move past me without usernames.
We are not friends. They stand in profile, their secrets their own.
They pass me. I have logged out but I am switched on.

Mod: You are now logged out of FriendRoulette. Log in as somebody else or exit?

A: Exit.

Mod: Remain logged in next time?

A: No.

Mod: Preferences remembered. You are logged out. You are home.

Blackout.

A: What's your pleasure?

B: Fun.

A: What's your poison?

B: I want to taste you.

A: I'll be your poison. I'll let you drink from me.
B: Bet you taste sweet.
A: I do. Come taste what rivers here.
B: It's wet.
A: It's warm.
B: It is warm.
A: Can you smell it?
B: Yes.
A: Smells like flowers.
B: Smells like nectar.
A: Smells like poison.
B: Smells real.
A: Come. Drink deep.
B: Tasty.
A: Swirl in me. Come in me.

Buzzing Saffy

A translation of Sappho's 'A Hymn to Aphrodite'

I.
Sister, on your precious throne of metal bling,
funking daughter of jagged skies and lightning,
domme of odes, listen close now, come on. Sister,
  I'm woman calling.

Listen how you listen, catch my morning buzz,
my voice carried over wire and horizon,
just come, as you came before. Sister, leave your
  strobe-light happening.

II.
Your arrival is the tide-ripple of doves,
ecstasy's muscle-rhythm through the club.
You lift high over skies, glow stick bright, throw down
  heavens to hip-wind.

The haters still come. And you—my avatar,
cover girl, superstar—wait while I sulk! Quick,
blow kisses when you text back. Spit me a rap, girl,
  I need your reply.

III.
You will say: Who has dissed you this time, sister?
Who stole your pissed off heart? Can you take it back?
They'll soon give all that you gave, then give you more.
  They always return.

Tell me who to petition, who to burn out,
who to placard—you promised me this, sister.
Come now. Keep your vow. This world could soon be ours.
  Be my damn lover.

MICHAEL ATKINS

BIOGRAPHY

Michael Atkins is a writer, anthropologist and drag queen from Birmingham. He currently lives in Manchester, where he undertook his PhD. The sequential art that follows is a comic strip taken from his PhD thesis.

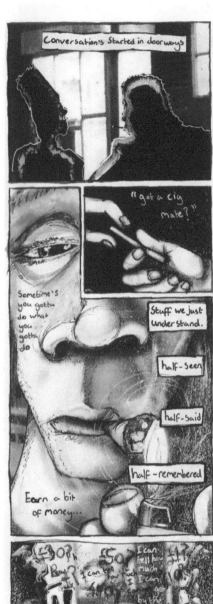

Rylan Cavell

Biography

Rylan Cavell puts his talents to many uses. Between working as Original Fiction Editor for *Starburst Magazine*, hosting the Gay Agenda radio show on Fab Radio International and putting on performances of his own stage-plays he attempts to have a social life and earn a living. He can often be found sat at his computer, tea pot within reach, hammering away on the keyboard like there's no tomorrow. He counts Hans Christian Andersen among his heroes, and can't leave a book shop empty handed. His to-read pile is growing considerably faster than his have-read pile.

Rylan can be found on twitter @therylancavell and his website, bewilderbeastlyproductions.co.uk.

WOULD YOU CHANGE

Gladys Bentley enters.

GLADYS BENTLEY
    Well those are some sour faces. You could curdle milk.

HARVEY MILK
    I'd rather they didn't.

GLADYS BENTLEY
    Beg pardon?

HARVEY MILK
    Harvey Milk. Nice to meet you.

GLADYS BENTLEY
    Likewise!

Gladys shakes Harvey Milk's hand enthusiastically.

QUENTIN CRISP
    Mr Crisp.

GLADYS BENTLEY
    Pleasure. I'm Gladys. 'America's Greatest Sepia Piano Player',
    'Brown Bomber of Sophisticated Songs'. *(chuckles)*
    Gladys Bentley.

QUENTIN CRISP
    The singer?

GLADYS BENTLEY
(amiable chuckling)
    The one and the same! The one and only! I feel a little zesty.
    Feelin good. Suppose you folk don't feel it though?

SAPPHO
(morose)

> We have had the pleasures of the afterlife denied us. We lay in
> the cold earth, slowly falling away to stark white bones in the
> dark of damp soil. Grinning skulls. That is where my smile
> lies now. Not upon my lips. Never more upon my lips.

GLADYS BENTLEY

> I wouldn't mind a-laying upon those lips. Sure I could make
> you smile, doll.

Sappho looks at Gladys, a strange look on her face.

SAPPHO

> Is that so?

GLADYS BENTLEY
(chuckling loudly)

> Why so glum? So we're dead? Couldn't get much worse
> could it?

HARVEY MILK

> I wouldn't be so sure. You heard what some say lays in wait
> for 'sinners'?

QUENTIN CRISP

> Folly, fantasy and fabrication, my dears. It would appear that
> the Powers That Be have decided upon this setting as the
> scene for some posthumous performance. I for one, refuse to
> disapoint.

SAPPHO

> Four chairs. Four of us.

HARVEY MILK

> What's this all in aid of?

QUENTIN CRISP

> I suppose, Mr Milk, that the answer to that question will be made clear once we have satisfied whichever deity has placed us here.

GLADYS BENTLEY

> This is one strange situation, and no mistake.

HARVEY MILK

> Seconded.

Tint enters, carrying four slim brown card folders containing a few typed pages each. Each one is named. One for each of the main cast.

TINT

> Oh you're all here!

GLADYS BENTLEY

> I sure am.

Gladys slaps her belly.

GLADYS BENTLEY

> Wouldn't wanna leave any of this behind.

TINT

> Right. Well, I'll bring in the refreshments. I've been assigned as your case worker. Rather last minute. Peripheral inconsistencies, you see.

HARVEY MILK

> I don't see. Case worker? What case?

TINT

> Your case. You collectively have been assembled because of your unique perspectives.

SAPPHO
Our perspectives? Explain.

TINT
(indicating each in turn, Milk, Sappho, Crisp, Bentley)
Campaigner. Uninhibited. Affectations. Denial.

SAPPHO
And our being here does what? Aids what? To what end have
been   been collected here?

TINT
Ripples. Insubstantial and tiny, but radiating, growing, rebounding. This room affects the whole of creation.

A gong sounds.

TINT
Sorry! I've been summoned.

Tint moves to exit, depositing the four files on the nearest chair.

HARVEY MILK
Hang on! You can't just drop that bombshell then dash off.

The gong sounds again.

TINT
Gotta run. Sorry. That gong means another religious war has kicked off! Humans! *(rolls eyes)* Ha!

Tint exits.

The cast stare after Tint. Confused and unsure.

SAPPHO
>This room affects the whole of creation?

Sappho grabs a magazine from the table and tosses it across the room.

SAPPHO
>What effect do you suppose that had?

Harvey Milk glances at the magazine.

HARVEY MILK
>For the whole of creation? Not much. But it looks like someone called Katie Price is having a bad time.

GLADYS BENTLEY
>It's a bunch of balony! Gotta be.

HARVEY MILK
>I wouldn't be so sure.

QUENTIN CRISP
>Affectations? Whatever was meant by that?

Quentin Crisp takes up the file with his name on.

HARVEY MILK
>Do you really think we should be poking about in those? You don't know what might be written—

Sappho takes up her folder and reads some of the content.

QUENTIN CRISP
>Mister Milk, there hasn't been a thing written about me that I have not read. Good, bad and downright lies. I find much of it riveting, imaginative fiction. So I see no reason why I should cease that habit for the mere reason that I've popped

my clogs.

SAPPHO
(searching through her file)
>Why us? Why us four? Entirely disconnected . . . What is it
>that ties us together?

HARVEY MILK
(suddenly realising, finds it amusing)
>Thinking about it, it's a little obvious.

SAPPHO
>Not to me. Would you care to enlighten us?

HARVEY MILK
>I think it's because we all represent some aspect of homo-
>sexuality.

SAPPHO
>Oh such a barbarously hybrid word. How ugly. Why mix
>Greek and Latin like that? Homosexuality?

QUENTIN CRISP
>Homogenic, Uranian, queer, lavenderist . . . Sapphist. Take
>your pick. They all apply and mean similarly: The love and
>lust and desire for a partner of the same gender as one's self.

SAPPHO
(closing and discarding her file)
>Why would that connection bring us all here? There is
>nothing more natural in the world . . .

GLADYS BENTLEY
>Don't you believe it, honey. Problem is, the world changes.
>One freedom arrives, another vanishes. Progress is made in
>one direction, then people pull in the other. Eternal tug-of-

war, with no-one ever truly winning.

SAPPHO

The freedom to love? Who would dare deny the freedom and the right to love? The heart cannot and should not be governed by laws and parchment and men sat in conference! I give my love to whomever I desire. I have written extensively on the topic. Who would dare be so monstrous as to try and govern the heart?

GLADYS BENTLEY

I blame religion. World is governed by rigid old men in dresses and starched collars.

SAPPHO

What religion?

HARVEY MILK

Sadly, most of them, these days.

SAPPHO

So we have been collected here because of the people we loved. Tell me then, Gladys Bentley, why are you labeled as 'denial'? Did you deny yourself love?

GLADYS BENTLEY

I don't like to talk about it.

HARVEY MILK

I don't think we have much choice. Clearly the Powers That Be want something to come of our meeting. What, I haven't a clue, but if we talk about our experiences, it might shed some light.

GLADYS BENTLEY

I don't like talking about personal stuff to strangers.

QUENTIN CRISP

> We may be strange, but strangers, no longer. Ms Bentley, kindly indulge us. Answer Sappho's question.

SAPPHO

> Denial? Explain, please.

GLADYS BENTLEY

> The short answer? I made myself live a lie. Not always. Oh there were some wonderful days during the prohibition. Alcohol was illegal you see, so these underground pockets opened up. Dens of iniquity... *(chuckling)* Oh they were the best days. I performed! Sang my heart out, raised the roof! I played the Joanna too. Thumping the keys and thumping out a mean tune. Made up my own lyrics to some popular numbers. Raunched them up a fraction. The crowd liked it when I got a little cheeky.

QUENTIN CRISP

> I would very much have liked to visit these places. I grew up in London as the bombs were falling.

GLADYS BENTLEY

> Funny you should say that. We were awaiting our own bombshell. And me; my own. Y'see, we were safe. In our hidden world we could relax. We could be anyone we wanted to be, and we could be who we really were. The dark corners and dingy bars were a safe haven. Oh you should have seen it. Mr Crisp, you'd have loved it. When I performed I wore such an outfit! Bet you ain't seen the like. Pristine white top an' tux. Not a usual look for a big black beauty, hey?

QUENTIN CRISP

> Unique. Your style was impeccable.

SAPPHO

> You had your freedom. What lie were you living?

GLADYS BENTLEY
(avoiding the question)

> . . . I flirted with the ladies in the crowd. We were very accepting back then; in the speakeasies. People from all walks of life want to drink and a dance. They could find both, and a whole heap more with me. The speakeasies . . . I tell ya. Ain't nothing quite like 'em. But it ended.

HARVEY MILK

> Prohibition ended?

GLADYS BENTLEY

> It all ended. Then there was the Great Depression, and the Second World War . . . But not before I'd got married though. *(long, deep sigh)* She was beautiful. Skin like cream, and eyes so bright . . . Not legally binding o'course, but we were so in love . . . Nothing lasts forever. I was a fool to think it would.

SAPPHO

> It is not foolish to believe in love everlasting.

GLADYS BENTLEY

> I was a fool. What I did. The way I behaved. I panicked.

SAPPHO

> When stung with love, though the pain and ecstasy of it may fade, that scar will remain. A woman should bare it with pride!

GLADYS BENTLEY

> I wish I'd heard words like that back then. I may have done things differently.

HARVEY MILK

What happened? After prohibition ended, after it all ended?
What did you do?

GLADYS BENTLEY

It's all so strange in hindsight. Looking back from here it's
like a roadmap, you know? Whatif Backalley, Might-
havebeen Boulevard, Ifonly Avenue. Which turnings I
took, which ones I probably should have taken . . .

QUENTIN CRISP
(quoting)

'I shall and ages took the difference.'
be telling this with a sigh. Somewhere ages hence: Two
roads diverged in a wood, and I—I one less traveled by, And
that has made all the difference.

GLADYS BENTLEY

Quote Frost all you want, I took the other. The well
trodden, safe and predictable path. I squeezed back into the
closet.

QUENTIN CRISP

I'm surprised there was any room.

Gladys gives him an off look, thinking he is making reference to her girth.

QUENTIN CRISP

Every closet door I opened, I was told 'get away, there's no
room in here.' I have very much found the closets are all full,
and bursting at the seams.

SAPPHO

Closet? You went and hid in your wardrobe?

HARVEY MILK

It's an expression. It comes from . . . actually where does it come from?

All shrug or shake their heads.

HARVEY MILK

Well, anyway, to be in the closet means to hide your true identity. To pretend to be someone or something else to fit in with the perceived norm.

SAPPHO

I don't think I would like it very much; this world of yours. It is so different from mine.

GLADYS BENTLEY

You can say that again.

SAPPHO

I shall not repeat myself.

GLADYS BENTLEY

I wanted to go mainstream. I wanted success and a big music career. My name in lights! And I got it.

SAPPHO

But at what cost?

GLADYS BENTLEY

I did a deal with the devil. Well, that's how it feels now. I started dressing as a woman again, but it felt like putting on a costume. It felt like taking a turn at drag. The top and tux boxed up and put away.

HARVEY MILK

Why didn't you just stay as you were?

GLADYS BENTLEY
> It wasn't an option.

HARVEY MILK
> It was always an option.

GLADYS BENTLEY
> Not for me. At least, it didn't feel like it.

SAPPHO
> What did your bride have to say on the matter?

GLADYS BENTLEY
> We separated. It wasn't a real marriage. It wasn't a 'holy union' between one man and one woman. We had such an argument. I called it an 'unholy union', I remember. The heat of the moment makes us   say stupid things. She was so sad. Never saw her cry before that day. Never saw her again after that day. Too late to do anything about it now.

SAPPHO
> So you sacrificed your own happiness, for some musical success?

GLADYS BENTLEY
> You make it sound so insignificant.

SAPPHO
> To me it is. Was it really of such importance to you that you threw away your love, and took to hiding? Hiding behind a mask of the 'perceived norm'.

GLADYS BENTLEY
> You can't make me feel any worse about it than I already do, doll.

QUENTIN CRISP

    If I recall correctly, did you not engage the company of a husband?

GLADYS BENTLEY

    You make it sound like a business transaction.

QUENTIN CRISP

    Well, that's what it was, was it not? Dressing like a woman, behaving like every other Dorris or Dierdrie... What's left to complete this picture of blissful, dreary, everyday mediocrity? A husband.

GLADYS BENTLEY
(angry)

    Why're you all turnin' on me? It's not like I hurt you, It's not like I harmed any of you. As far as I can see the only one I hurt in this whole picture... is me. So yeah, I had a husband. We had a good life. Wasn't what I wanted. But I couldn't have what I wanted! To know that the life you lead, that the life you enjoyed so damn much isn't there anymore, isn't allowed, isn't permitted. Imagine it. Everyone talking down to me, condescending to the dirty dyke. It's bad enough the attitude people have cos I'm black. Just think what it'd be like if they learned that not only that, a lesbian too! With a faux wife! We'd be hunted. We'd be chased out of town. That's the real world. That's the picture of blissful, dreary, everyday fear, dear. You try telling me you faced the same prejudice as a black person. A black woman. A gay black woman! It's not something I did on the toss of a coin. It was hard. It ruined me.

QUENTIN CRISP

    It is occasionally my intention to tease but never to offend.

GLADYS BENTLEY

    You're a sharp old silver-tongued snake, and you need to

watch what you say.

QUENTIN CRISP
I shall keep my words more guarded in future.

GLADYS BENTLEY
See that you do, and we'll have no more beef.

SAPPHO
You had your freedom, and gave it up. You have all my sympathy.

GLADYS BENTLEY
What good's your sympathy gonna do me? Gotta live with my own mistakes . . . well . . . I lived with my own mistakes.

Gladys takes up her file and opens it.

GLADYS BENTLEY
What's this damn thing say about me anyhow?

She flicks through a couple of pages, then finds a photograph.

GLADYS BENTLEY
Oh.

HARVEY MILK
What is it?

GLADYS BENTLEY
A photograph taken on my wedding day.

QUENTIN CRISP
Forgive me for asking: which wedding day?

GLADYS BENTLEY
The only one that truly meant anything to me. We look so

happy. Atlantic City, that's where we were married. She meant the world to me.

QUENTIN CRISP

I have always recommended limiting one's involvement in other people's lives to a pleasantly scant minimum. That way neither they nor you can ever be disappointed in the other.

GLADYS BENTLEY

You've a weird way of seeing the world, you know that?

INDEX OF STORIES